VENUS MARS

P. Khurrana has been pursuing the subjects of astrology, mantras, numerology, sun signs, vaastu and tarot with great passion, over the years. Columnist, author and a devotee of Lord Shiva, he has featured as an astrologer on television channels such as India News, Live India, Zee News, ABP News and Big FM (92.7). He is often invited for the muhurats of Bollywood films and is an advisor to many actors and business tycoons.

To know more about the author, log on to www.astroindia.com

VENUS MARS
Love *and* Marriage

P. KHURRANA

RUPA

Published by
Rupa Publications India Pvt. Ltd 2021
7/16, Ansari Road, Daryaganj
New Delhi 110002

Sales centres:
Allahabad Bengaluru Chennai
Hyderabad Jaipur Kathmandu
Kolkata Mumbai

Copyright © P. Khurrana 2021

The views and opinions expressed in this book are the author's own
and the facts are as reported by him which have been verified to the
extent possible, and the publishers are not in any way liable for the same.

All rights reserved.
No part of this publication may be reproduced, transmitted,
or stored in a retrieval system, in any form or by any means,
electronic, mechanical, photocopying, recording or otherwise,
without the prior permission of the publisher.

ISBN: 978-93-90260-18-8

First impression 2021

10 9 8 7 6 5 4 3 2 1

The moral right of the author has been asserted.

Printed at Thomson Press India Ltd, Faridabad

This book is sold subject to the condition that it shall not, by way
of trade or otherwise, be lent, resold, hired out, or otherwise circulated,
without the publisher's prior consent, in any form of binding
or cover other than that in which it is published.

Dedicated to my late parents
Smt. Raj Khurrana
and
Shri R.D. Khurrana

Those who know astrology only indicate what might take place in future. Who else, except the creator Brahma, can say with absolute certainty what will definitely happen?

Contents

Foreword   *xi*
Preface   *xiii*

1. Venus   1
2. Mars   26
3. The House of Love and Marriage   39
4. Marriage Focus on Other Planets   52
5. Matching Horoscopes   63
6. Some Yogas   83
7. How to Perform a Wedding Ceremony   110
8. Issues in a Marriage   121
9. From the Astrologer's Desk: An Outlook on Case Studies   133

Acknowledgements   151

Foreword

Marriage counselling is a complicated affair. On the one hand, it is the most popular and constructive aspect of astrology, while on the other, it raises the question of thwarting any possible planetary impact. It also involves the question of the significance of marriage itself. What is the meaning of harmony in marital life? What is the purpose of marriage as an institution? The modern trend of unconventional marriages also needs to be taken into account, and above all, the astrologer should also be very clear in his/her mind as to what he/she is striving to achieve. Is he/she trying to warn his/her client of the impending danger, or is he/she going to indicate the possible consequences and adjustment problems likely to be faced in a given marital partnership? What are the possible difficulties in marriages and how can the contracting parties deal with those difficulties? And above all, what is the meaning of marriage itself from a deeper standpoint? These are some of the questions that astrologers ought to be aware of before venturing into the realm of marriage counselling.

A recent trend among some Indian astrologers is to relate a large number of natal charts of married partners or of contracting parties, indicating their personal weaknesses and justifying them on the basis of astrological or planetary combinations. If someone has been indulging in an extramarital relationship, there must have been some planetary combination leading the person to that situation. But could there be any other implication of such combination which, if known by the person concerned, could lead him/her to overcome those difficulties? It is indeed a duty of the (Hindu) astrologers who are capable of comprehending the planetary impulses on an individual's intimate life, to find out the deeper implications of those forces and how the individual could transmute those physical conditions (or sexual impulses) towards a higher end.

Therefore, the task of marriage counselling is indeed an onerous responsibility, which P. Khurrana has been discharging with conscience and sincerity. He has brought out this marvellous book as a practical guide for astrologers and for every human being to bring harmony in the lives of the suffering souls at the behest of Venus and Mars.

The author deserves to be thanked for having chosen the subject 'Venus-Mars: Love and Marriage'. This book portrays clear-cut guidelines to help the masses match horoscopes for marriage.

Guru Swami S. Chandra
Spiritual guru

Preface

Venus and Mars are the only planets that play a very important role in family bliss. Any chart may have most of the planets in beneficial positions, but a couple will not enjoy marital bliss only if Venus and Mars are malefic. How far you will enjoy physical and mental comfort with your partner depends upon the placement of Venus and Mars. Of course, the study of Jupiter is also equally important.

Those who understand the accurate position of Venus and Mars will agree that my approach makes the process of searching for a suitable match much easier if followed and understood properly. In addition, most couples will be able to lead a very happy, successful and long married life with this advice.

Matching charts for marriage has its own scope and also limitations. A chart that shows loss of spouse within months or a year or two after marriage, can benefit from astrological counselling through matching and manage to push the eventuality to a reasonably distant time in the future. Since a chart is bound by Karmic parameters, matching cannot bring out miracles. However, it can be an effective tool to fight premature loss of spouse and minimize other problems that occur between spouses.

The present practice of matching of horoscopes is faulty and misleading. I have observed in certain cases that there is good compatibility, but *Bhav Melapak* is absent, resulting in unhappiness in marital life. On the contrary, there are cases where the horoscopes are weak in compatibility, but marital life is quite happy if *Bhav Melapak* is present. Most of the astrologers attribute Mars (Mangal) for an unhappy union. It is better not to match the horoscopes merely on the basis of Mars being in an unhappy House.

There are cases where it has been found that in spite of a tally of 30 gunas out of 36, with no dosha, the couple is leading a miserable married life. In another case, the tally of gunas has resulted in a happy married life. Such cases have disappointed the believer in astrology. The reason is that matching has not been done properly, say, in terms of mental affinity, sexual compatibility, domestic happiness, etc., for one reason or the other. I sincerely believe that wise and judicious matching of horoscopes can lead to a fairly stable and happy marriage. I use the word 'fairly' because no marriage is perfect—just as no man upon earth is perfect—save for the great souls, sages and incarnations.

In this book, I have focussed on the study of Venus and Mars, but the readers must accept the changing concepts in matching horoscope. I have brought out various aspects about matching of horoscope and astro-analysis into martial happiness.

1
Venus

This planet is beneficial, gainful negative, attractive and temperate. It is the planet representing love, relationships, pleasure, beauty and art. Its day domicile is in Libra and night in Taurus. Its exile is in Scorpio and Aries. Its exaltation is in Taurus and tall is in Virgo. This planet is often referred to as the Lesser Fortune.

Its metal is copper and day is Friday. In a layout of cards, it indicates the woman, the female.

This planet makes the native gentle, generous, loving and happy, with a liking for pleasure and comfort. Physically, he is gifted with fine features and is well formed. Venus makes the native somewhat self-centered since he wants pleasure for himself to be of topmost priority.

It results in ailments of the chest and the generative system mainly due to overindulgences.

VENUS IN THE HOUSES

Venus in the 1st House

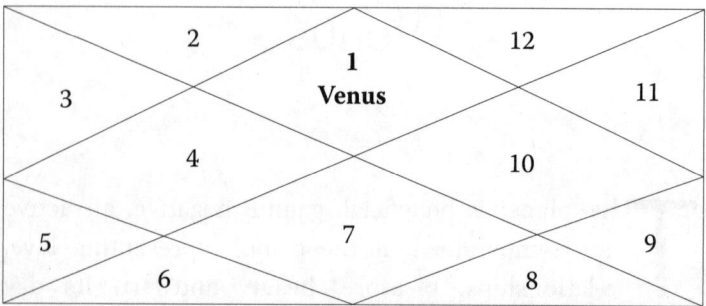

Venus placed in the 1st House exercises a beneficial influence over the entire life of the native, unless afflicted. It bestows qualities such as a gentle and affectionate temperament, good manners and a love and appreciation for the aesthetic and artistic.

The native shall enjoy good health and will lead a long life unless Mars throws an adverse aspect, in which case, it would cause severe illnesses resulting from overindulgence in pleasure and comfort.

With an adverse influence, this key in the 1st House brings many affairs of the heart, disloyalty and problems of the chest and spine.

Astro advice: *Give grains to a white cow.*

Venus in the 2nd House

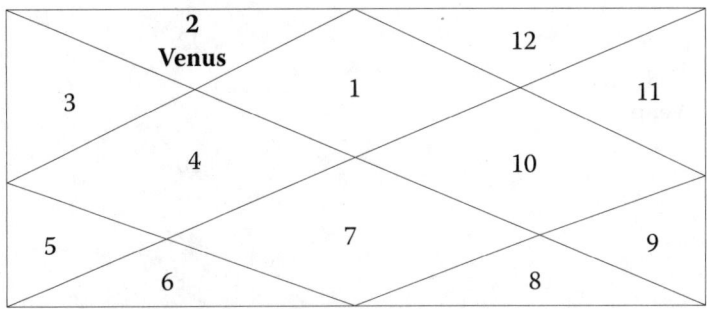

This is a beneficial situation for business ventures, unless placed in an unfavourable sign. The native shall enter into a matrimonial alliance with a rich partner who will also keep him happy and he will be proper in all fields. The 2nd House being the House of personal worth bestows definite aesthetic sense, and if the 3rd House is favourably situated, these artistic inclinations shall lead to fame and fortune.

This does give the native a tendency to splurge on himself and others. He likes expensive garments in pastel or light-wear. He also has a desire to be of assistance to other people who are rich, happy, cultured and of a high status.

In a woman's chart, this position is not that favourable for matrimony since the spouse is an incorrigible spender, flirt and gambler.

Astro advice: *Offer sugar, rice and dairy products at a place of worship on a Friday before 11.00 a.m.*

Venus in the 3rd House

```
            2              12
  3                 1
Venus                            11
            4              10

  5                 7
            6               8           9
```

This position showers domestic accord and takes the native on many pleasure trips. The native shall have refined education, unless there exist some adverse aspects.

He shall have a penchant for beauty and culture. This placing is for writers. This position makes the native prefer unknown people over family members. However, he shall always be in cordial terms with them.

In the horoscope of a woman, the planet in the 3rd House signifies an encounter with a cultured man while on a trip. The alliance may not be monetarily gratifying, however, shall be of high social status.

Astro advice: *Your lucky jewels are diamond, topaz and high-class light-coloured stones.*

Venus in the 4th House

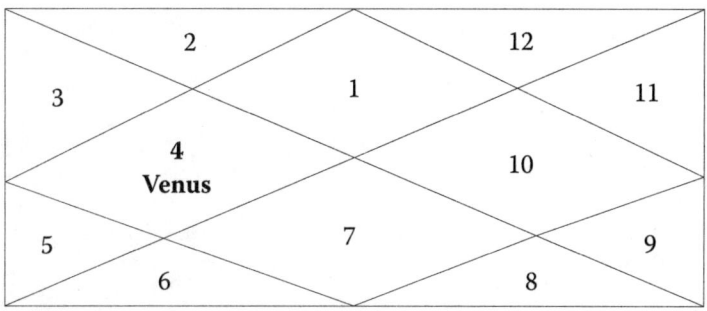

This enables the native to get continuous joy and peace at home. His abode shall also be done up in exquisite style. There is also the definite indication that the native shall receive money, property or inheritances from either his mother, wife or other women.

The native shall enjoy a carefree, happy and long life. If Mars or Saturn is on evil aspect with Venus in the nadir of the heavens, it implies that the mother or wife may pass away early and unexpectedly.

Astro advice: *Fondness for pets must be avoided.*

Venus in the 5th House

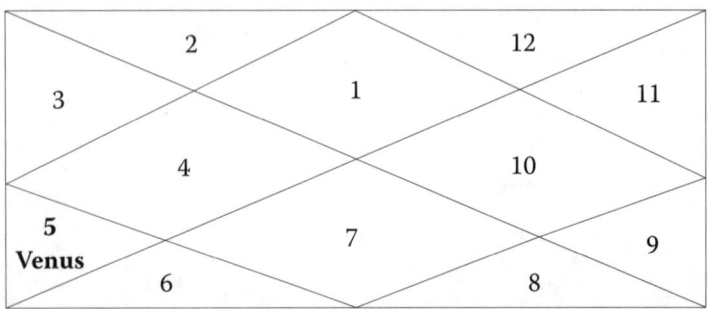

This is the true placing of the planet and herein it holds a strong influence over pleasure and feelings. It bestows a liking for socializing, happiness, friends, generosity, love and balanced thinking. It is fortunate for taking risks, betting speculations and a big family, particularly girls. However, this is possible provided Saturn is not adversely aspected with Venus.

The planet, if dignified in the 5th House, gets monetary prosperity in an artistic profession or it might make the native interested in things related to recreational places.

For females, this situation is an indication of early love intrigues. If influenced adversely or not well positioned, the planet may bring disillusionment in matters of the heart.

Astro advice: Donate silver, milk and rice in a temple.

Venus in the 6th House

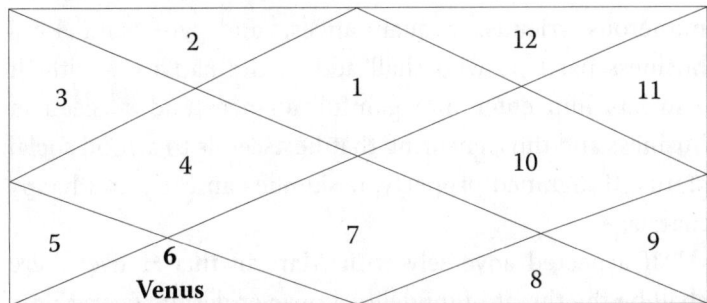

In the 6th House, the planet is not very significant with reference to health issues and is definitely not beneficial for the same, particularly for Pisces, Scorpio or Cancer.

When dignified, it is good for home life, which shall be happy and peaceful. It also signifies loyal and truthful workers. This position is favourable for uncles and aunts and might lead to a legacy from a relation.

Astro advice: *Prayer to Sri Laxmi or Sri Durga is apt.*

Venus in the 7th House

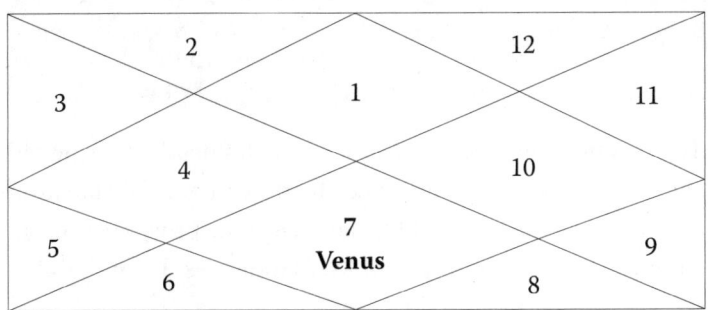

This is a highly beneficial situation being in the House of Unions, the planet being the ruler of love. It bestows numerous friends, acquaintances, and wise and loyal business partners who shall add to the native's wealth. It also lets him enter into gainful alliances and succeed in business and thus, ensuring that he ascends to a good social status. If dignified property, it signifies an early and happy marriage.

If aspected adversely with Mars in this House, there shall be the threat of infidelity, however despite everything, the partners shall not separate.

Astro advice: *Prayer to* maghalakshmi *and puja to* panchamukha deepam *(a lamp with five wicks) is beneficial.*

Venus in the 8th House

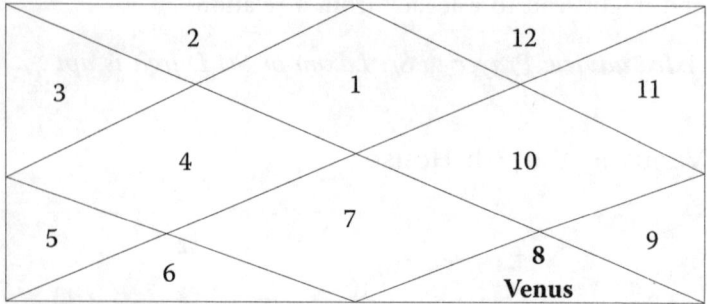

The position ensures a peaceful and calm death at a ripe old age. It also favours inheritances from women. This position also indicates a favourable marriage and prosperity in all spheres. An adverse aspect of Mars indicates the probability of loss of spouse. An aspect of Saturn shows the possibility of an alliance with a widow/widower.

Astro advice: *Give proper respect to your in-laws.*

Venus in the 9th House

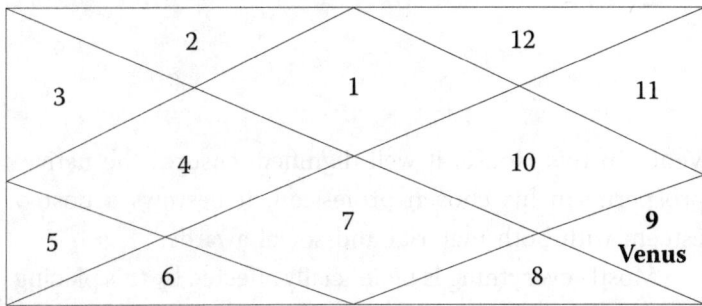

This situation is beneficial for mental matters and long trips. It signifies marriage with a foreigner and even if this does not happen, the alliance shall always be with a rich and intelligent person. The position bestows a liking for philosophy and theology, particularly in families.

Astro advice: *Donate seven grains to a Brahmin lady.*

Venus in the 10th House

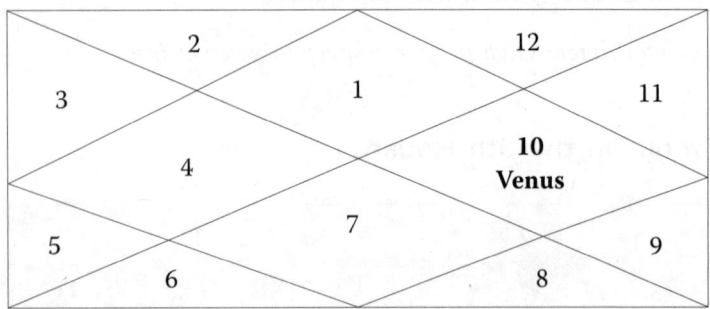

Venus in this House, if well dignified, ensures the native's prosperity in his chosen profession. It bestows a post of esteem with both material and social awards.

Mostly everything is beneficially affected by this placing. Fame and fortune are given to the native in good measure, provided Venus is strongly placed. If the opposite is true, than there shall be problems related to females.

Astro advice: *Immerse four square pieces of silver in flowing water.*

Venus in the 11th House

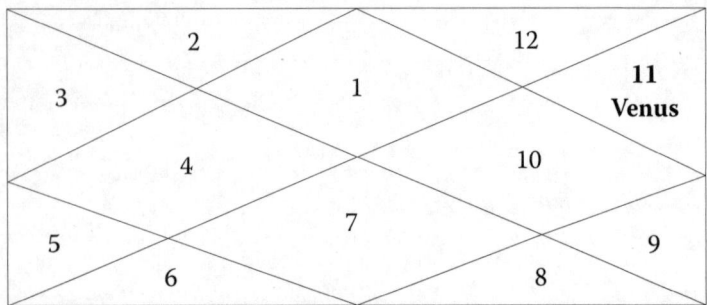

The native shall be assisted by many powerful acquaintances. The planet in this House is also beneficial for offsprings who shall be strong and beautiful. It also endows the native with popularity and particularly with women who shall enable him to rise in society.

Astro advice: *Donate silver at your place of worship.*

Venus in the 12th House

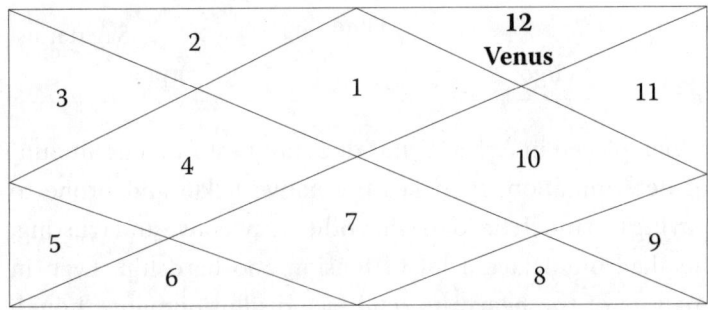

The planet is not favourably positioned in this unlucky House since it takes the native towards those people who are of a low status and it also indicates vague and dishonourable professions and affairs.

It may result in estrangement from the spouse because of rumours, particularly if Venus has an adverse aspect from Mars. This is not favourable for health of the native since it causes infections and illnesses.

Astro advice: *Donate sugar, rice and white cloth.*

VENUS IN THE SIGNS

Venus in Aries

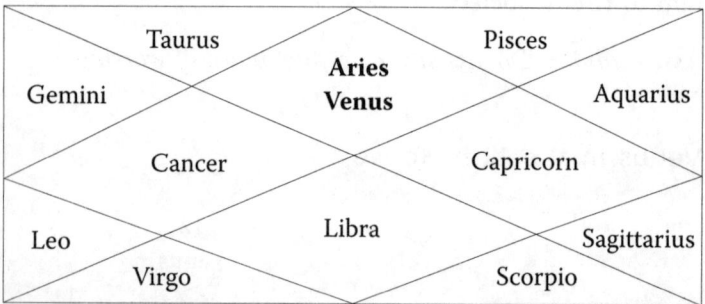

When placed in Aries, Venus does not bestow a fair amount of determination. It makes the native fickle and prone to paying too much heed to what others say. Naive and trusting, he shall often face a lot of tension and hardship. Even in matters of the heart, he shall face disillusionment, though the situation does favour marriage at an early age.

When in 10 of Aries, Venus indicates a marriage that does not meet the native's wishes and leads him to bear this burden while craving for release. This release may take place. If the Moon is in bad aspect with Mars, then the demise of the spouse might occur and also, pave the way for a second marriage. If the planet is favourably aspected by the Sun, it indicates the exact opposite.

When in 20 of Aries, the planet leads to the estrangement of the partners since the tastes and ideas of the partner and the native are not in accordance with one another. This is more so in a female horoscope, in which case, it indicates an aggressive and crude husband, particularly if an adverse aspect is cost by Mars.

Astro advice: *Avoid alcohol and non-vegetarian food.*

Venus in Taurus

Gemini	**Taurus Venus**	Pisces	Aquarius
	Aries		
	Cancer	Capricorn	
Leo	Libra		Sagittarius
	Virgo	Scorpio	

When situated in its own domicile and aspected beneficially, the planet is favourable for matrimony since it achieves a balance between the heart and the mind. If adversely aspected, then it signifies a changeable but gentle mate. The planet in conjunction or square with Mars in Taurus indicates problems in matters of the heart. Favourably aspected Venus is an indicator of prosperity in all matters. It brings good fortune and enjoyment in all the issues ruled by the House in which it is situated.

When in 10 of Taurus, Venus is a symbol of matrimonial infidelity. It indicates envy and an alteration of love and feelings.

When in 20 of Taurus, the planet is an indication of

excessive ardour. The native adores one who does not reciprocate and as a result of which, he feels tense. If Saturn afflicts with Venus, it signifies grief. With an aspect at the Moon or Mercury, particularly in the 3rd House, it signifies a trip related to love, but this may not bring about the desired result.

Astro advice: *Give water to the rising sun.*

Venus in Gemini

	Taurus		Pisces	
Gemini Venus		Aries		Aquarius
	Cancer		Capricorn	
Leo		Libra		Sagittarius
	Virgo		Scorpio	

When in this sign, the planet brings a number of acquaintances. The native is liked and loved by everyone. However, he may not be as profoundly loving and this may break a few hearts. It is also a symbol of infidelity in marriage or that the native is the object of affection of two people at the same time. Venus in Gemini is also a sign that the offspring shall be beautiful and if the 5th House is beneficial and the Moon is favourably situated and aspected, the native shall be blessed with twins.

When in 10 of Gemini, the planet is a symbol of indecisiveness and changeability in matters of the heart. Also, it indicates worry due to a beloved as well as envy.

When in 20 of Gemini, the planet and the situation is much better. It indicates the chance of prosperity and progress in issues ruled by the house in which Venus is situated. It signifies amicability, loyalty and fame.

***Astro advice:** Get up early in the morning and touch the earth with your right hand.*

Venus in Cancer

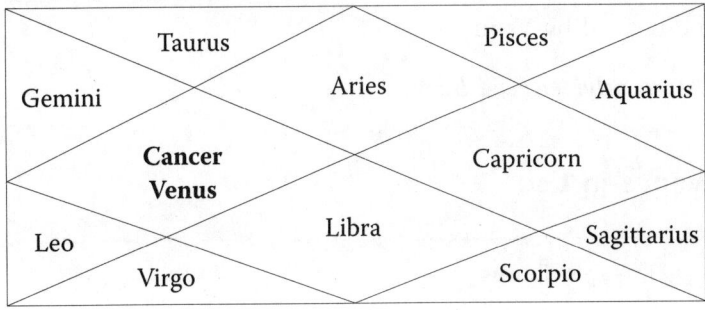

Venus situated in Cancer is not a favourable position. It signifies unfaithfulness, changeability and secret liaisons. An adverse aspect of Mars brings about estrangements from the spouse and it might be an indication of entering into matrimony with either a divorcee or a widow/widower. It does not favour accord in marriage and is the reason for arguments, particularly if the Moon is in evil aspect and if the planet is in the 4th House. If the planet is favourably aspected, it indicates prosperity but no emotional richness. Venus, strictly speaking, may not bring sadness in the affairs of the heart, but it does make the native get easily bored, which is why he causes greater grief to others than to himself.

When in 10 of Cancer, Venus indicates in all certainty, estrangement from the spouse. It also signifies threat of mishaps or injuries due to reasons related to love, particularly if Mars emanates an adverse aspect to Venus.

When in 20 of Cancer, it gives the native the ability to conquer difficulties in love and be happy despite everything, even if it means taking an aggressive stand which is beneficial in some alliances, especially if the mate is strongly influenced by Venus.

Astro advice: *Feed birds.*

Venus in Leo

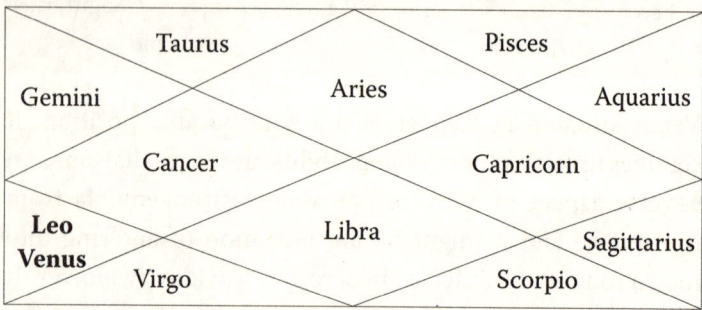

The planet situated in this sign is beneficial for an early marriage, unless it is affected by adverse aspects. The alliance shall endow happiness, respect and contentment to the native. This is true even with adverse aspects; however, in that case, the alliance is short-lived as boredom and tiredness soon set in. The native or his mate are oblivious to what life is all about and wish to know it better (particularly in 20 of Leo). This will, therefore, result in many irritations and arguments, which shall be hard to resolve.

When in 10 of Leo, the planet symbolizes loyalty and the matrimonial alliance shall cease only with the demise of the one of the mates. However, if Mars sends out an adverse aspect, there shall be fights. However, these shall not last for long since the partners will be bound by immense physical attraction.

Astro advice: *Immerse oil in flowing water.*

Venus in Virgo

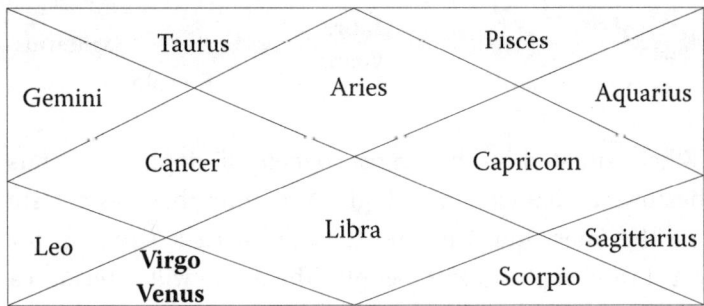

Venus placed in Virgo is not beneficial for marriage. It brings strange notions about love, which is more physical than emotional. An adverse aspect of Mars, Saturn or the Moon may signify sexual perversity.

This placement creates singles such as nuns, monks, spinsters and bachelors. If Saturn aspects Venus, it may result in sex disorders.

When in 20 of Virgo, the planet is not beneficial for matters of the heart. It signifies an alliance with a rich but much older person and this causes trouble to the native later on since Venus, herein, signifies moral isolation.

Astro advice: *Worship any devi (goddess).*

Venus in Libra

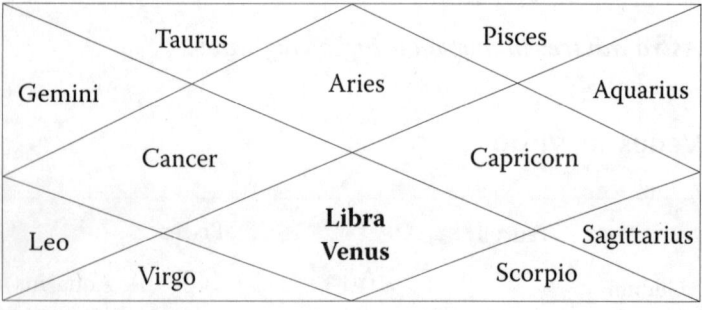

When situated in her most beneficial domicile, Venus bestows a character of a high order, one that has a taste for the finer things in life. It is the perfect situation for artists and sophisticated people. The native will enter into a financially and socially enriching marriage which shall bring joy, unless the Sun is in conjunction with Venus, in which case, it indicates early estrangement. Like it happens with many marriages, this shall not take place without resulting in a lot of envy and hatred from people around the partners. However, favourably aspected, they shall remain satisfied and happy.

When in 10 of Libra, this situation is highly fortunate for a man. It shall enable him to ascend great heights by virtue of his own luck and intellect. Herein, the planet lets the native take risks and do anything since he is led by love and achieves prosperity.

When in 20 of Libra, the planet signifies steadiness. However, an adverse aspect of Mars to Venus shall bring tension with reference to the offspring, particularly if this takes place in the 5th or the 11th House.

Astro advice: *All family members must give food to cows.*

Venus in Scorpio

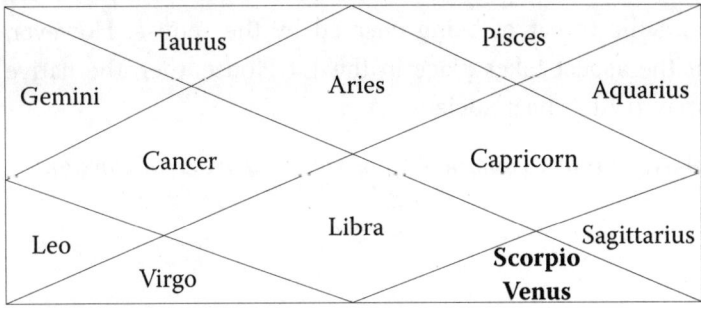

Venus's situation in Scorpio (one of Mars domicile) is not beneficial. It results in numerous problems and difficulties with reference to issues ruled by the House. In the 5th House, it might bring about the demise of the offspring. In the 6th House, it indicates ailments of the generative system. In the 8th House, it signifies the early death of the wife. When situated in a female's horoscope, it indicates serious disillusionment in matters related to love and emotions and is frequently indicative of the deception and loss of trust in a girl's life. If Venus is aspected by the Moon in the 4th House, it signifies a child born out of wedlock.

When in 10 Scorpio, the planet signifies arguments between the marriage partners, estrangement and a second marriage, which will probably be as bad as the first one. When in a man's horoscope, it signifies that he shall be involved in many affairs and shall cheat on his partner, and if Mars aspects Venus, it signifies that he will have a mishap of some sort.

When in 20 of Scorpio, it indicates unfaithfulness, arguments and unpleasantness in marriage. When in the 7th House, it brings about dishonour, estrangement, court cases and the threat of being cheated by the spouse. However, if the aspect takes place in the 1st House, then the native may try to cheat society.

Astro advice: *Donate 7 kg of rice in a place of worship.*

Venus in Sagittarius

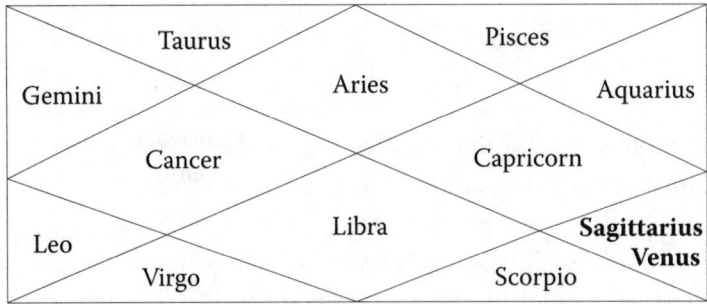

Venus placed in Sagittarius is highly beneficial for eminent artists as it shall shower wealth, fame and honour. However, it is not beneficial for matrimony. Marriage is delayed and may take place even if there is no love involved, and if adversely aspected by Mars, it shall bring disrepute.

When in 10 of Sagittarius, the planet results in profound love being more important for the native rather than passion. This life shall be enriching both from the financial and emotional point of view, provided Venus is not afflicted.

When in 20 of Sagittarius, Venus signifies a matrimonial alliance of convenience rather than love. Venus, if aspected by Mars and in the 8th House, signifies widowhood or marriage with one whose spouse is deceased.

Astro advice: *Give food to a blind beggar.*

Venus in Capricorn

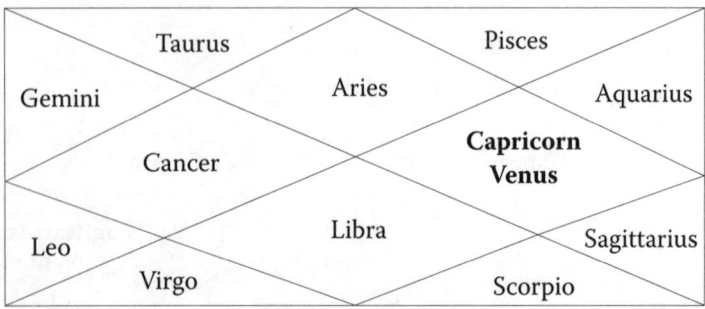

When situated in Capricorn, Venus is not beneficial for either love or matrimony. It makes the native highly changeable and strange in matters of the heart. If the planet is favourably aspected, particularly in the 7th House, the native shall be married to an older person of a Saturian temperament and the home shall be sad and devoid of children. If Mars casts an adverse aspect and Venus is in the 5th House, then the offspring shall pass away at an early age. Venus in Capricorn also brings about arguments between the spouses.

When in 10 of Capricorn, the planet brings peril with reference to women. An adverse aspect of Saturn may result in death because of sadness, particularly in a woman's horoscope, or, if indicated by the chart on the whole, death may occur due to suicide with Mars, Venus and Saturn in square aspect and Venus being placed in this decanate in the 8th House; when in 20 of Capricorn, the situation is much better. The problems related with love persist and the desolation remains, but there is no threat of death since the determination of the native bounces back even after disillusionment in matters regarding love and affection.

Astro advice: *Give proper respect to your elders.*

Venus in Aquarius

	Taurus	Pisces	
Gemini	Aries		**Aquarius Venus**
	Cancer	Capricorn	
Leo	Libra		Sagittarius
	Virgo	Scorpio	

Venus situated in Aquarius is not beneficial for the native's struggle in life since it bestows a feminine and lazy temperament, too much generosity or even fragility. If the horoscope is lucky, the placement of Venus shall be favourable and signifies that the native shall have a stable, happy life. If the sign is placed in the 4th House, the domestic scenario will be peaceful, calm, somewhat stable and filled with accord and this is what the native wants.

But if the horoscope depicts hardships, then Venus is not beneficial since it shall result in the estrangement of the married partners due to the native's feebleness. Unfaithfulness and secret liaisons may take place, which may result in the loss or gain of money depending upon how Mercury is positioned and aspected.

When in 10 of Aquarius, the planet is unfavourably placed. With reference to love, it signifies cheating and deceit. This shall favour the native financially to some extent.

When in 20 of Aquarius, the situation is more favourable and will bring favours and gains that shall be more enduring in nature and will be brought about by the assistance of an individual of the opposite gender.

Astro advice: *Keep your distance from bad company.*

Venus in Pisces

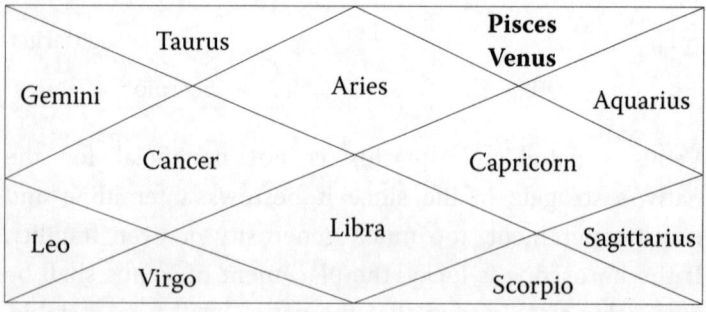

Positioned in Pisces, the planet signifies that the native shall marry early and also that there will be two marriages. For a man, if the sign is situated in the 8th House, it indicates that he will lose his wife to death early in life. For a woman, it implies that she will have a much older man as her spouse and he will pamper her thoroughly. Financially, the situation is favourable since Venus in Jupiter's domicile is devoid of any affliction and showers good fortune, thereby allowing the native to prosper in all his ventures, particularly in angular House.

When placed in 10 of Pisces, the planet loses a few of its good qualities since it indicates arguments caused by lies and cheating in love affairs. It brings about unfaithfulness and estrangement. It may also result in the loss of status if Venus is afflicted by Uranus, in which case, ill luck will be related with the particular House.

In 20 of Pisces, the planet showers immense joy on the home. It brings accord between partners, healthy offspring and a comfortable financial status. However, all this depends upon the fact that there are no adverse aspects.

Astro advice: *Wear a diamond on you ring finger.*

2

Mars

MARS IN THE HOUSES

Mars in the 1st House

If Mars is in the Ascendant, the native will be quarrelsome, devoid of means of livelihood and also suffer from blood diseases. The native is lean and emaciated in body, and generally living separately from his wife and children.

Notes

This position signifies an instinct of domination, more especially over others than over oneself. It also means moral and physical courage if Mars is well aspected. Otherwise it may indicate cowardice and cause the native to attack those who are weaker than himself. It is often a sign of quarrels and disputes. The tarot card represents the Man, the lover. It donates success through industry and activity and also through personal merit. The ascendant also prophesizes an event of a sentimental or passionate nature. In this House, it gives energy, vitality and great expenditure of the Life Force.

Astro advice: *To increase your magnetic vibrations, you should wear all shades of red, crimson and gold.*

To make yourself more fortunate, you should give gur (jaggery) to monkeys on Tuesdays. Also, throw empty earthen vessels in flowing water.

Mars in the 2nd House

If Mars is in the 2nd House, the native will be deprived of the pleasure of his wife, wealth and children. Though the native is brave, the spouse will be unattractive, miserable, cruel, powerless, evil-minded and indebted.

Note

With Mars situated in this House, the native will have uncontrollable inclinations towards extravagance. His appetites being considerable, it will be necessary if the balance is to be maintained, that he should be endowed with a corresponding amount of wealth. This will induce him to earn money through his own efforts and exertions. With Mars well aspected, he will have many potent ideas, which will never allow him to be anything from the narrow standpoint. His activity will be overflowing, but often muddling. There will be the lack of system, but this will be compensated by a good memory and inborn sense of organization. Moreover, Mars in this House makes a leader, and his usual subordinates will be influenced by Mercury or Jupiter, which will mitigate the mistakes of their chief. It is a fortunate position when Mars is well aspected and placed in one of his own signs. If Jupiter sends a good aspect to the 2nd House, the native will contract a wealthy marriage, which while may not fulfil his emotional desires, will give him complete satisfaction from the monetary standpoint.

Mars badly placed in this House, with bad aspects from Uranus or Saturn, will cause many troubles and unavoidable pecuniary losses.

Astro advice: *To make yourself more fortunate, you should wear transparent Burmese ruby (weight 6 ¼ to 10 ¼ ratti) to be fixed in gold and to be worn on a Sunday before 8.00 a.m. after Pran Pratishtha. You will be enthusiastic in everything you attempt.*

Mars in the 3rd House

If Mars is in the House of brothers, the native will be blessed with wealth, luxurious vehicles, jewellery, gems, tentage, etc. and is free of diseases, etc. He is beautiful, bold and wealthy.

Note

Mars in this House will be the cause of quarrels with those surrounding the native; violent disputes will arise, and there is even the danger of blows and wounds. Harmony between brothers and sisters is far from perfect, the native being impetuous and desirous to have the upper hand at all costs. As there is the probability of the parents being similarly inclined (genetically), peace is impossible. The native's mind is critical and he may, education permitting, become a first-class politician, a leader. This position is not good for travelling. It causes accidents, or even through beasts of burden, if Saturn sends a bad aspect, and these will be due to the native's own recklessness.

Astro advice: *To increase your magnetic vibration, you should wear all shades of green, white and orange.*

To make yourself more fortunate, endow wine/spirit to the rising sun. It is also suggested to keep a black-colour pet dog.

Your lucky jewel is red coral (moonga) of 8 ¼ ratti in silver ring, which is to be worn on a Tuesday evening after sunset in your ring finger after Pran Pratistha.

Mars in the 4th House

If Mars is in the 4th House, the native has long legs and long hands, is patient in the battlefield and of stout body. He is cruel, poor and always in debt.

Note

Mars in this position causes the premature death of the spouse. It is always a sign of approaching danger in an ordinary laying out of cards. In the horoscopes, it implies disorders of the circulation, and a domineering and despotic character, which interferes with domestic harmony. This position also presages a risk of destruction of house/property by fire, especially if the Sun is in bad aspect with Mars. This planet in the nadir of the heavens is usually a sign of sudden death, following a heart attack or an accident. If well aspected, Mars may increase the inheritance through work and exertion. If afflicted, it shows continual troubles in life.

***Astro advice**: To increase your magnetic vibration, you should avoid black and dark colours.*

Your lucky jewel is ruby of 6 ratti, which is to be worn in silver on a Sunday morning in the ring finger after Pran Pratishtha.

It is suggested that one should not accept any bribe, gift or grant. Also, you must give red clothing or utensil in charity.

Mars in the 5th House

If Mars is in the House of intellect, the native talks less, becomes a duffer and is deprived of the pleasures of wealth, valour and employment. He suffers from cough and bloated stomach.

Note

This indicates a disorderly life, lacking in organization. The native, who is more often than not an unfortunate gambler or speculator and whose fortune rapidly dwindles, lives from hand to mouth. It is an indication of activity in the pursuit of pleasure, with little zest for serious matters. There is danger for the children, who will suffer from diseases of the nature of the sign in which Mars is situated. In the case of women, an evil aspect will point to trouble connected with childbirth, and if it comes from Neptune, there is the danger of miscarriage. If Mars is dignified, it makes children active but will be difficult to train. They will be naughty and independent, but will have every chance of success in life.

Astro advice: *To increase your magnetic vibrations, you should wear all shades of red and crimson as well as dark colours. Your lucky jewel is ruby and diamond, which are to be worn according to the specification mentioned by the author earlier.*

You are suggested to give away utensils of silver, gold and copper in a place of worship.

Mars in the 6th House

If Mars is in the House of diseases, the native overpowers his enemies, is beautiful, enjoys wealth and respect from others, is respected in his family and pays due respect to others, but not to the family of the maternal grandfather. He, however, suffers from some vice.

Note

Mars badly aspected in this House and situated in a bad sign, can induce fever and inflammation of that part of the body ruled by the sign in which this planet is placed. If, on the contrary, it is well aspected, Mars denotes considerable physical resistance, which will render the native immune to diseases.

This position favours the acquisition of money, and the

constant improvement of the home surroundings from a material point of view. Badly placed or aspected, it causes numerous disputes with servants and employees.

Mars in the 6th House often indicates robbery with violence on the part of someone employed in the home, to the detriment of the consultant, or his uncle and aunts. With Scorpio in the 5th House, Mars influences more, especially those who take care of their fellow creatures.

Astro advice: You should wear all shades of gold, orange, golden brown and blue.

To make yourself more fortunate, you should give a large quantity of foodgrains, especially wheat, in temples or charitable institutions.

Your lucky jewels are moonga, diamond and glistening stones.

Mars in the 7th House

If Mars is in the 7th House, the native is deprived of normal opportunities of sexual contacts with his wife and the facilities of health, wealth and house. He suffers from theses wants as well as of a conjugal life.

In this House, Mars confers a great amount of sexual passion, thus causing an early love affair or marriage. Well aspected, this planet inclines to a wealthy marriage with a woman who will not rule at home, and who will be of the marital type, with all its virtues and vices. In the absence of good aspects to Mars, the couple will not have much chance of staying united, especially if the Ascendant contains a feminine planet, as this causes friction in the home, due to the indolence of one of the marriage partners, and the excessive activities of the other. This position also denotes loss of the marriage partner and is bad for contracts and partnerships.

If well placed and receiving a good aspect from Mercury, Mars in this House is a sure token that the native will undertake big things, which will bring along appreciable gains, a trail of envy and jealousy, as well as endless lawsuits.

Astro advice: *Take things a little easier. Do not let others play your game. The real silence is control of emotions. Prayer to Lord Shiva or your Guru will bring you good luck. The favourable directions for puja is north-east. Wear a gold chain. Sunday is a favourable day.*

Mars in the 8th House

If Mars is in the House of death, the native will be harsh-tongued and deprived of conjugal happiness. He will remain ever anxious about something or the other, suffer from wounds, inflammation, venereal diseases and impurity of blood. He has a lean body and is an expert jeweller.

Note

When Mars falls in this House, it indicates violent death or, if it is in aspect with the Sun or the Moon, the death of the father or mother. If the aspect is a good one, the native will benefit from it. An aspect with Venus may also mean the sudden death of the spouse, who is of a domineering and violent disposition.

In a horoscope in which Saturn, Uranus or the Moon are afflicted, Mars in the 8th House shows the possibility of suicide.

Astro advice*: One should wear all shades of gold, yellow or red.*

To make oneself more fortunate, one should give spirit and water to the rising sun and chant the mantra 'Aum Aan Aangarkaaye Nameh' 108 times daily.

Your lucky jewels are high-class moonga and diamond. These should be worn in the ring finger only after Pran Pratishtha.

Mars in the 9th House

If Mars is in the 9th House, the native commands respect in the court of kings, is respected by all, loves other women, enjoys happiness in his social circles and spends his time in aimless journeys.

Note

In the 9th House, Mars, if it is dignified, provides good chances of success for the native, as it makes him enterprising and energetic, from the physical as well as the mental standpoint.

He is gifted with a fine mind, which enables him to

take a broad view of things, exactly as they are. While this position is often the sign of struggle, it also promises success if the sign occupied by Mars in the 9th House is powerful. If the case is the contrary, and if Mars is afflicted, it brings up a tendency to neurasthenia, depression, lack of self-confidence and often misunderstanding with regards to the parents. In this House, Mars inclines towards travelling.

Astro advice: Partnership of any kind will be favourable with the opposite sex, especially if partner's name starts with the alphabet B, S or A. A high-quality diamond or moonga will be your lucky jewel. Have regular check-ups for all your ailments. Puja to panchamukha deepam or worshipping a devi (goddess) will bring good results. South-east is a favourable direction, particularly for females.

Mars in the 10th House

If Mars is in the royal House, the native is wealthy, intelligent, honest, diplomatic, economical, respected by his people, courageous, bashful, fond of ornaments, well-dressed and charitably disposed.

Note

The power of Mars in the mid-heaven is great, if it is dignified. It favours the most hazardous experience, and these can be carried to a successful issue. This position may be that of a political leader, or a dictator; it enables the native to overcome his enemies, and all kind of snares.

Difficult times will often occur, numerous struggles will be his lot, but he will be able to defend himself, and if the horoscope generally is good, he will obtain power and authority through strife. This position does not go well with a subordinate post. The native will be an undisciplined solider, or an employee who cannot submit to his employer's authority, unless he is given a great deal of latitude. When Mars is dignified in the 10th house, it brings success to women, but may cause misunderstandings on the part of the mother.

If Saturn is situated in the 4th House, it will mean premature death of the father, and may also indicate a relatively untimely death for the native. Mars in the 10th House always makes the native violent.

If the position and aspects of Mars are unfavourable, this position in the 10th House may cause the worst catastrophes, from imprisonment to accidental death.

Astro advice: *Prayer to Sun God (Surya Dev), Lord Shiva or Hanuman will bring excellent results. Left-handed people with this combination should worship any devi (goddess).*

Lucky jewel is high-class ruby, moonga and yellow sapphire. Favourable direction is south.

Best days for prayer are Tuesday and Monday.

You should offer gur (jaggery) or wheat in a place of worship.

Mars in the 11th House

If Mars is in the 11th House, the native wears dresses of silk, velvet, brocade and other costly material. He is valiant, provided with horses, elephants and other conveyances, maintains servants, has no enemies, is intelligent, truthful and possesses vigour during sexual intercourse.

Note

This is usually an evil position. It indicates numerous disputes and even physical violence with friends or social acquaintances. It means disagreements between the parents and their children, and will cause their loss if Saturn occupies the 5th House, and casts an evil aspect.

If dignified in the 11th House, Mars will provide power, and will make a leader who is more feared than loved; but for this to happen, the Sun, Venus or Jupiter must be in good aspect. Mars is the planet of ambition, and it will thus attain its high aims, but not always without causing sorrow to others.

Astro advice: The tendency to change prayers and worship must be curbed. Repetition of Gayatri Mantra or puja of Sat Naryana is beneficial.

Those suffering from insomnia or slight stammering in speech should offer ghee, red clothes or utensils at the place of worship on Tuesday in the evening. Your lucky jewels are diamond and all red glistening stones. Recite the mantra 'Aum Aan Aangarkaaye Nameh' for 108 times after sunset.

Mars in the 12th House

If Mars is in the 12th House, the native uses harsh language with his relatives which hurts them. He also causes them agony by being atrocious, angry and ever troublesome.

Note

In this House, Mars often exhibits a credulity approaching stupidity, so that this position causes great difficulty. There will be scandals, or unfaithfulness, if Venus is affiliated in the 7th House. If Mercury occupies the 7th House, it means trouble with the law, and may cause imprisonment for the native. If the Moon is afflicted in the 9th House, the native may end his days in a lunatic asylum. In this House, Mars cannot be fortunate, and the least harm it can do is to cause danger through an accident or operation.

Good aspects from Jupiter, Venus or Sun may mitigate the difficulties, which will be constant and numerous, but without which the consultant would predict life to be drab and purposeless.

Astro advice: *To overcome unexpected loss of money or accident, you must gather foodgrain, red wine and copper coin that weigh as much as you and immerse them in flowing water in midday. Your favourable day is Tuesday. Your favourable direction is north. You should avoid black colour. The ring of eight gems in eight metals will prove beneficial.*

Recite the mantra 'Aum Aan Aangarkaaye Nameh' for 108 times after sunset.

3

The House of Love and Marriage

MARS IN THE 7th HOUSE AND MARITAL MALADIES

The 7th House indicates all about the husband or wife in any birth chart. The 8th House rules marital happiness, life of the partner and *saubhagya* (good luck) in a female nativity. The influence of Mars on the 7th House for males and the 7th and 8th houses for females, produces adverse results with respect to marriage and marital life.

Mars in the 8th House for males is not as damaging for married life as in the 7th. Mars in the 8th House may cause injury, accidents, blood impurity and infection, operation, cuts, burns, boils and danger to life such as assassination or unnatural death. For females, Mars in such position creates marital disharmony, widowhood, discord, denial of conjugal bliss and all kinds of physical problems to the spouse.

My observation about the adverse effect of Mars with respect to marital life is quite different from that of established rules for Kuja Dosha. Mars in the 8th House should be considered as causing heavy Kuja Dosha for females, whereas for males, it does not cause such strong dosha. Similarly, Mars in the 2nd House is adverse for females with respect to marital life because it aspects the 8th House. This is not so bad for men.

In the case of males, the 7th House should be under the influence of Mars either by occupation or by aspect, Mars in the Lagna, the 4th, the 12th and the 7th houses gives rise to Kuja Dosha for males. For females, Mars Dosha exists when Mars is in the 1st, 2nd, 4th, 7th and 12th houses. I just want to prove that Mars in the 4th House for females gives rise to a strong Mars Dosha, as it then aspects the 8th.

At the time of matching of horoscopes, Kuja Dosha should be given due importance. In the case of a female, Mars in the 5th House should be considered as causing Mars Dosha, but a 5th House Mars cannot be considered so in a male chart.

Chart 1: Birth Date: 11.2.1945

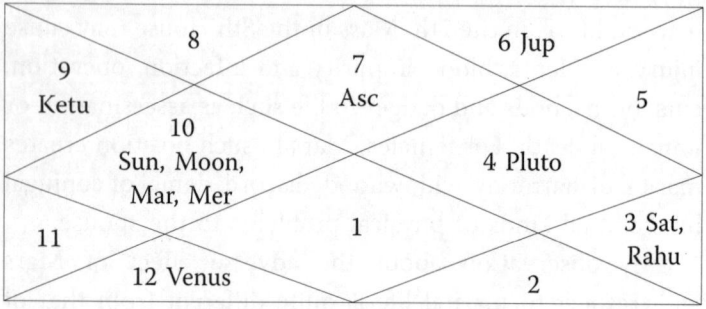

Kuja Dosha

The native of Chart 1 was born in Virgo Ascendant with Mars exalted in the 5th in association with the 10th and Lagna lord Mercury and 11th Lord Moon. The combination of Mars, the Moon and Mercury in the 4th House receives the benefic aspect of Jupiter. There is no malefic aspect on the 5th House. Venus is exalted in the 7th, whereas the 7th Lord Jupiter is in the Lagna. Apparently the horoscope shows that she must lead a happy and long-lasting marriage. But it was not so. She got married on 2.5.1964 to a smart and handsome person. A daughter and two sons were born. Differences between the couple started soon after the marriage. The husband started having affairs and the native got a legal divorce. After the divorce, she married a Muslim man. The marriage lasted for seven years.

The native was extremely happy, but the second husband left her and got married to another. The native suffered a lot of humiliation and anxiety. Mars is the Lord of the 8th and 3rd and joins the 5th. As such, it should have affected children and health of the native, but here, it resulted in marital disasters, suffering and humiliation which spoiled her status in society and family. This can be attributed to the heavy Kuja Dosha caused by Mars in the 5th House though in his sign, he might have had the Kuja Dosha balanced.

Chart 2: Birth Date 20.4.1951 at 11.21 p.m. at Ramnagar

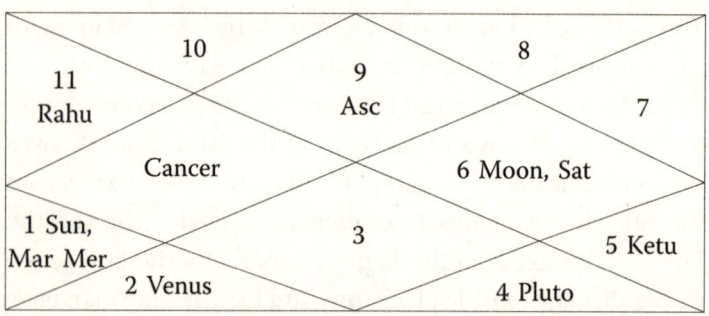

Extramarital Affair

Chart 2 is of a native born in Sagittarius Ascendant with Mars, the Sun and Mercury in the 5th. Mars is in his own sign Aries and the Sun is also exalted there. The native got married to an Indian Administrative Service (IAS) officer at an early age. Three children were born, but the husband got involved in extramarital affairs and divorced the native. In spite of very strong efforts, the native could not get any kind of marital happiness. Saturn also aspects the 7th House. Thus, the 7th and 8th houses are both damaged. The aspect of Mars and Saturn of the 12th is also adverse, but the worst affliction is of Mars in the 5th, leading to legal separation.

Chart 3: Birth Date 26.5.1971 at 2.00 p.m. in Lucknow

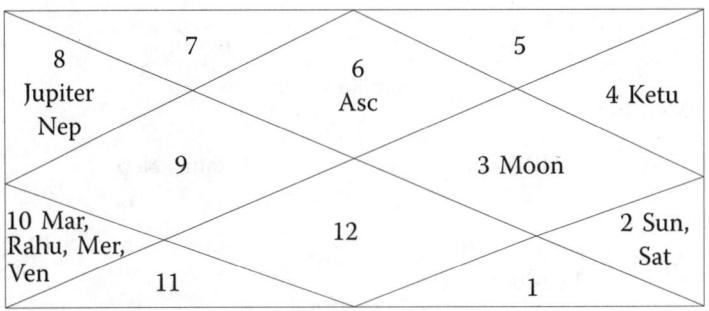

Marital Disharmony

The native of Chart 3 was born in Virgo Ascendant with exalted Mars in the 5th and the ruler of 7th Jupiter is in aspect. The 8th is occupied by Mercury and Venus. The aspect of Mars on the 8th caused a lot of havoc in her life. She was married on 27.4.1992. A daughter was born on 1.7.1993, but the husband left her before that. The husband has not visited her even once since then in spite of the repeated efforts of her family. She is working in a reputed organization and earning a good salary. The reason for the marital disharmony is the position of Mars in the 5th.

Chart 4: Birth Date 26.12.1951 at 4.08 p.m. at Lansdowne

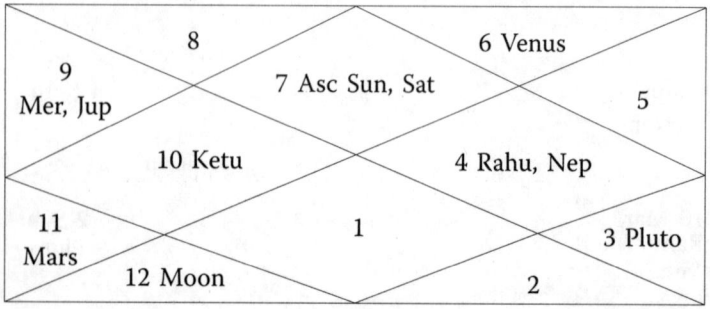

Marriage Denied

The native of Chart 4 was born in Taurus Ascendant with Mars, Saturn and Ketu in the 5th House. The Moon and Mercury are in the 7th. Thus, there is an exchange between the lords of the 5th and 7th houses between Mars and Mercury. Jupiter aspects the 5th and the 7th house. The native could not get married at all. There are many other reasons for this, but I just want to show that the affliction of Mars denied the native marital happiness in spite of Jupiter's aspect on the 5th and 7th house.

Chart 5: Birth Date 9.11.1924 at 5.25 a.m. at Chandausi

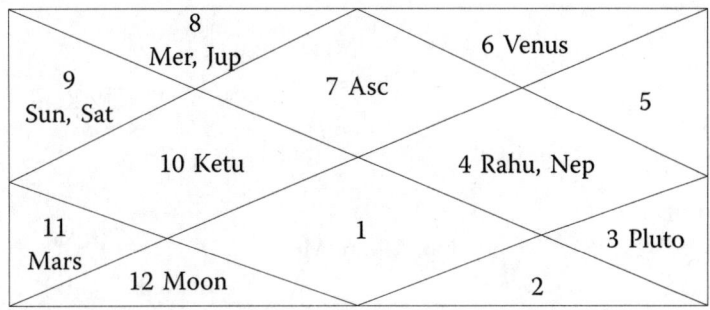

Widowhood

The native of Chart 5 was born in Libra Ascendant. Mars is the worst planet for Libra borns, as it owns the 2nd and 7th houses. Mars in the 5th is extremely bad. The 7th is aspected by the Sun and Saturn and the 8th by Mars. Jupiter and Mercury also aspect the 8th which improves the 7th House to a great extent. Even then, the affliction due to Mars in the 5th led to her getting married to one who was 10 years older than her and had lost his first wife. Married life was extremely unhappy. Eight children were born, but none of them was affectionate or caring. She lost her eldest child and also suffered widowhood when she was 44 years old.

Chart 6: Birth Date 2.11.1959 at 8.30 p.m. in Allahabad

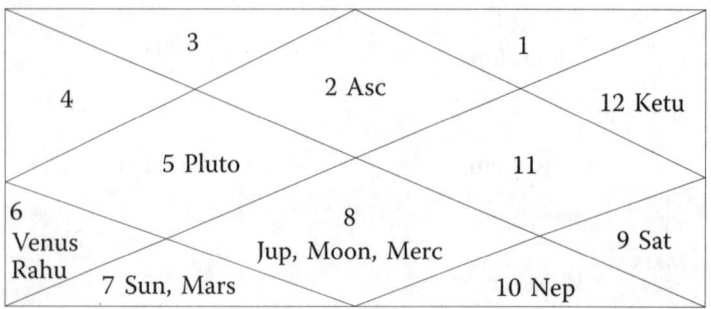

Separation

This is the horoscope of an extremely talented girl who obtained brilliant result in the IAS exam in 1984. She got married on 27.12.1984 to a smart and good-looking IAS officer. The rank of the native was much higher than that of the husband. This led to conflicts and their living separately. The intervention of the girl's father only added to her problems. Both finally separated. She is completely deprived of conjugal life.

The 6th and 11th Lord Mars in the 5th in Libra is responsible for such adversity in her married life. Mars aspects the 8th. The 8th Lord Saturn is in the 7th. The 7th Lord Jupiter is in the 6th in association with the Moon and Mercury, 2nd and Lagna lord respectively. Thus, both the 7th and 8th houses are adversely afflicted. The Lord of the 7th Jupiter falls under Papa Kartari Yoga being hemmed between first rate malefic Mars and Saturn. In Navamsa,

Saturn in the 7th in opposition to Venus is also quite adverse. There are many good Yogna in the birth chart such as all the eight planets in continuation from the 3rd to the 7th House. But Mars in the 6th in association with the Sun has destroyed her marital life. This is not only due to Saturn in the 7th but also because Mars is in the 5th aspecting the 8th House.

My observation on Mars in the 5th in the horoscope of a female are as follows:

1. This position of Mars should also be treated as Kuja Dosha and as such taken into consideration while matching horoscopes for marriage.
2. Mars in the 5th may result in the untimely death of the life partner. It may also cause accident, physical harm, injury, serious operation, etc., to the life partner. Heart trouble or brain haemorrhage can also not be ruled out if Mars is afflicted, provided the 8th House is affected by evil planets in it.
3. Mars in the 5th may result in separation of the life partner soon after marriage due to serious difference of opinion and dissatisfaction over various aspects of life.
4. One may be denied conjugal bliss or not get married at all for one reason or the other.
5. One may be deceived in love life.
6. The life partner may get involved in extramarital liaisons, and therefore, desert the native if Mars joins the 5th House and there is no support to it in the husband's birth chart.

7. One may face a setback to marriage due to absence of physical pleasure.
8. Certain problems in connection with children may also be there such as the birth of only female children, unhealthy children, surgery and the like, but I am not touching on these here as I intend to show the malefic effects of Mars in the 5th House in respect of conjugal harmony only.

As far as my humble opinion is concerned, Mars in the 1st, 2nd, 4th, 5th, 7th, 8th and 12th houses for females should be considered as causing Kuja Dosha in the birth chart, whereas Mars in the 1st, 4th, 7th and 12th should be given importance as causing Kuja Dosha in the horoscopes of males. Kuja Dosha will arise only if the 7th House is aspected by or occupied by Mars in the case of males. In the case of females, the influence of either by position or aspect should be present on the 7th or 8th House. I have studied a number of male horoscopes where Mars is in the 8th and the wives have no Kuja Dosha, leading happy conjugal life. I find after an examination of hundreds of female horoscopes where Mars is in the 8th that they suffer marital disharmony if there is no cancellation of Kuja Dosha in the husband's horoscope.

MARS IN THE 12th BHAVA

This Bhava signifies expenditure, travelling, sexual pleasure, purchasing power, enjoyment, sleeplessness, etc. Due to Purna Drishti on 7th Bhava Mars becomes directly responsible for hindrance in marital happiness, health of spouse and dissipation. Mentality to oppose Bandhu (brother, friend, relation) develops. There is a decline of control over sex life. The native tends to veer towards cruelty, fault-finding, contemptuousness, gossip-mongering and courting trouble with others. The natives of this Yoga are excessive eaters, short-tempered, rebellious and argumentative. There is wealth loss and poverty in life. There is an excessive fury of agonies and maladies such as accident, suicide, headache, migraine, blood complaints and indigestion.

According to Kalyan Verma, the native is impatient, corrupt, disgraced, prone to cruelty and murder. However, one is not considered a strong Mangalik if Mars joins the 12th House. Only 50 per cent dosha of Mars should be taken into account while weighing Kuja Dosha.

The number of malefic results are maximum in Scorpio and Capricorn. In Aries, Leo, Sagittarius, Cancer and Pisces, the rate of malefic results are medium and in Gemini, Libra and Aquarius, it is less.

Nullifying Ill Effects: Some Opinion

Before making a final decision of Kuja Dosha on any native, the disposition and combination (the Yog) of all planets, Rashis and Drishti should be studied thoroughly in detail. A minute negligence in the study of the details will bring extremely fallacious predictions. In reference to Mangal Dosha, astrologers should always study deeply on the following combinations. It is widely believed that in these dispositions, there are no residual Mangal Dosha, as they get cancelled with the influence of benefic factors in the birth chart.

The following nullify the ill effects:

1. If Mars is in 4th or 7th Bhava and Aries, Cancer, Scorpio or Capricorn sign falls in these houses.
2. If Mangal is disposed with strong Moon, Jupiter or Mercury in Lagna, 2nd, 4th, 7th, 8th or 12th Bhava.
3. If Taurus or Libra sign falls in 7th or 4th Bhava having Mars.
4. If Gemini or Virgo sign falls in the 2nd House occupied by Mars.
5. For Leo Lagna, if Mars joins the 7th House.
6. If Mars of own sign is in 7th, 4th, 8th or 12th Bhava.
7. If Mars joins the 4th House identical with Libra or Taurus.
8. If 8th House Mars is in Sagittarius or Pisces.
9. If 12th House Mars is in Virgo, Gemini, Taurus or Libra.

Some observations based on my own experience are as follows.

According to many research scholars, there are many positions of Mars where the Kuja Dosha appears to be cancelled. These views vary from scholar to scholar, but my experience is that evils of Mars never get cancelled fully. The evils may, at the most, get reduced or minimized if corrective measures are taken. We have observed Mars doing harm in all positions. So, it is our sincere advice that we should not neglect Kuja Dosha. The intensity can and should be properly judged and weighed upon. For example, Mars in Leo in the 12th House will not be as harmful as Mars in Cancer in the 7th or 8th House. Evils of Mars or Kuja Dosha, as discussed earlier, are often wrongly understood by the common man that if a non-Mangalik gets married to a Mangalik partner, he/she will die as a result of that marriage. This is absolutely a false and misguiding view. If any of the partner dies or separation takes place, this does not necessarily mean that either of the couple has Kuja Dosha. There are many other combinations of planets leading to an unhappy married life, and discord and disharmony. We cannot blame Kuja Dosha for all cases of tragedy in married life.

Many writers have dealt with Kuja Dosha at length as applicable for each ascendant. An essence of that is presented in this chapter. These two points should always be kept in mind. First, the position of Mars, where this has been said to be cancelled, neutralized or becomes ineffective. If so placed, Mars comes in opposition to Jupiter or in association with Jupiter, the evils of Mars should be treated as many times increased. Several case studies have proved it.' The second point worth considering is the position of Saturn in opposition or in association with Mars. This will also enhance the evils of Mars. Under such conditions, rules of neutralization of Kuja Dosha do not hold good.

4
Marriage Focus on Other Planets

The first step is to get a thorough understanding of the individual horoscope in its relation to marriage. For this, we need to know the general influence of all the astrological factors in this connection.

In this case of marriage, there is a tendency to look towards the luminaries. Venus, Mars and the 7th House, and ignore everything else except such aspecting planets as there may be.

A very great number of positions of horoscope have a direct or indirect influence upon marriage. In separate chapters, I have given classified positions so that they may easily be referred to when any particular one is being examined.

It is often quite possible to discriminate between legal, illegal and irregular unions in the horoscope, although astrology is not concerned with man-made laws that differ in different ages and races. In normal cases, where the afflicting aspects are not of a serious nature will always result in a legal marriage. This is the natural course of events in our present civilization.

Serious afflictions in a horoscope will prevent marriage altogether, if they are sufficiently strong and involve barren signs. But if the signs occupied are fruitful ones and there appears to be a desire for marriage, the afflictions will tend to influence the conditions of the union.

Planets in Aries

Sun: An influential partner, or one of good birth or position. Marriage will bring friendship and may be brought about by a friend.

Moon: Secret love affairs, mysterious relationships.

Mercury: An intellectual partner. Many relatives by marriage. Marriage to someone from a distant land. A partner with weak health. Some secret feature with regard to the marriage.

Venus: A happy marriage, entered into hastily or in youth. Difficulty in restraining the affections, and danger of seduction or secret attachments. Risk attached to domestic affairs or danger of ill treatment from the opposite sex. Tends to cause unhappiness in marriage in a woman's horoscope.

Mars: Loss of money through marriage. Difficulty in consummating the union. For women, there is also a danger of seduction.

Jupiter: An ambitious partner. Gain through marriage.

Mental outlook and health changed by marriage.

Saturn: A jealous partner. Marriage to an elder or to a person previously married. Danger of poverty and trouble through marriage.

Planets in Taurus

Sun: Disputes or legal troubles through marriage. Liability to misplaced affection may form liaisons. For women, gain through marriage.

Moon: Secret love affairs. Gain or loss of money by marriage. Native will survive their partner.

Mercury: Worry, obstacles, difficulties. Loss in marriage.

Venus: Desire of self-control. Honourable love affair. Many troubles in love and marriage may be delayed. Financial loss in marriage. Death of partner. One union only. Quarrels may arise through incompatibility of temper.

Mars: Early love affairs. Loss of honour and scandal through attachment. Tragic or unfortunate marriage. Wife is the dominant partner.

Jupiter: Chaste affections. Gain through love affairs and marriage. Partner with mystical interests. For a woman, dangerous liaisons with a pervert.

Saturn: Strong passions. Danger or trouble through capricious women. Peculiar domestic experiences. Financial loss through marriage and death of the partner.

Planets in Gemini

Sun: To a woman, two love affairs or marriages.

Moon: Reprehensible conduct in marriage.

Mars: Involved in two simultaneous attachments. Marriage to a relative or a religious person. More than one union.

Venus: Desirous of spiritual love life. Dual love affairs, or attachment to a relative. Peculiar intrigues necessitated by home life with domestic ties. Attachment and marriage to a professional person. Partner may come from a place of considerable distance. Many relatives by marriage and successful affair in a distant land. More than one union.

Jupiter: Domestic sorrow. Marriage to a cousin or distant relative. Trouble in marriage through fickleness. More than one union.

Saturn: Marriage to a foreigner. An alliance made abroad or on a journey.

Planets in Cancer

Venus: Fickle and secret love affairs. Marriage may be delayed on account of money or occupation. Parents may help or hinder the marriage. Marriage to a person of better social standing or to one previously married, or to a foreigner. Partner with occult interests. Fame or notoriety through marriage. Death of the partner abroad. Union in a foreign country or during a journey or voyage.

Mars: Discontented partner, unhappy marriage which may bring scandal and ill repute. Struggle to maintain the home.

Jupiter: Fame, reputation or social success through marriage.

Saturn: Sorrow through love affair, domestic trouble and family discord.

Planet in Leo

Venus: Ardent, and may advocate free love. Secret attachments with inferiors which may lead to dishonour or failure in duty. Marriage to a friend or brought about by friends. A love marriage, sometimes following love at first sight. One lasting affection at the end of life.

Mars: Passionate love affairs and secret alliances. An ardent partner liable to disappointment in love, death of the sweetheart or partner. Separation or some irregularity in the union.

Saturn: The father helps or hinders a love affair. Marriage to a friend and realization of hopes through partner. More than one union.

Planets in Virgo

Sun: Position and reputation affected by peculiar liaisons.

Moon: Secret sorrow in marriage.

Venus: May cause celibacy. Strange or illegal loves, intrigues and tragedy in love affairs. Entanglements with inferiors, dishonour through dual attachments. Secret marriage or liaisons. Obscure partners or one with secret troubles. Partner helpful in financial affairs.

Mars: Danger of seduction. Peculiar ties. Unhappy affairs. Secret union with inferiors.

Jupiter: Secret love affair or marriage. Marriage to a social inferior which may involve or entail some peculiarity.

Saturn: Disinclined to marry. Romantic courtship. Trouble and loss through marriage. More chances of happiness with a widow than with a previously unmarried women. More than one union.

Planets in Libra

Sun: Strong influence for separation. Native often separated from partner, and usually the survivor. The partner will be a person of much strength, a source of help to native. For a woman, early engagement or marriage, but risk of trouble in connection with either or both.

Moon: Marriage may be hindered by a parent of the native or partner, perhaps a difference in age or social position. Favours marriage and popularity. Afflictions lead to separation and divorce. Liability to scandal and legal trouble. Danger to the reputation and position from vindictive women.

Mercury: Marriage for intellectual companionship with a clever, artistic or a literary partner. Sometimes, marriage to a relative, social inferior or poor person. Many obstacles and legal difficulties.

Venus: Pure and refined affection. Many sorrows due to the death of loved ones. Love affairs with relatives. A devoted partner, and a love marriage with financial sacrifices and heavy responsibilities, though sometimes, social advantage. Native survives their partner.

Mars: Strong influence for separation. Sorrow and trouble through love affairs. Marriage may be an early or hasty one, or greatly delayed through an early disappointment. Responsibilities through marriage, domestic strife. Danger to partner's life or health.

Jupiter: Happy and faithful marriage. Financial or social gains. Marriage may bring the 9th House matters into the life.

Saturn: May become celibate or suffer an early loss or disappointment. Father or father-in-law greatly influences the marriage. Partner differs in age or social position, and is often an inferior. Fickle fortune through marriage. Career may be greatly affected. If afflicted, separation and divorce.

Uranus: Hasty or early engagement or marriage. Danger of separation or divorce.

Neptune: Secret and strange love affairs. Treachery, deception and adultery. Danger of separation, divorce or annulment of marriage. Early bereavement, in cases of a happy union. Partner may be physically afflicted or could die under strange or horrible circumstances. May marry a foreigner or may be married in a foreign country.

Planets in Scorpio

Sun: For women, money or property by marriage. Danger of separation, or death of husband.

Moon: Favours marriage in a men's horoscope. For a woman, trouble through opposite sex, disharmony in marriage or trouble through other women. Money may be obtained through marriage, but trouble will accompany it. The wealth may be wasted or have to be spent freely on others.

Venus: Jealous in nature with strong passions. Dangerous attachments and risk of betrayal. Misfortunes through the opposite sex. An unhappy attachment may lead to suicide or murder. Partner might be previously married. Delay in love and marriage, loss of partner by separation or death. Money may come through marriage, but only after much trouble and difficulty. If Scorpio rises, or Venus is the ruler, most of the harm is caused by the native.

Mars: Gain by marriage. Partner will be unhappy. Danger of violence to or from the partner.

Jupiter: Critical or peculiar attachment. Unusual family experiences. Gain by marriage, and by the death of the partner. Liable to trouble or loss through the partner's actions.

Saturn: Sorrowful love affairs. Secret intrigues and domestic ties. Danger of venereal diseases.

Planets in Sagittarius

Venus: Love affairs affect reputation. Gain and spiritual improvement through marriage. Marriage to a relative, foreigner or person from distance. Marriage or union abroad or on a voyage. May cause secret love affairs and adultery. More than one union.

Mars: Spiritual improvement through marriage. Secret or often undeserved scandals. More than one union.

Jupiter: Gain through marriage. Two love affairs or marriages, one probably with a relative.

Saturn: Help or hindrance from relatives. Marriage causes travel or comes as the result of a journey. May lead to trouble or separation.

Planets in Capricorn

Sun: In a woman's horoscope, unfavourable for marriage and for husband's health.

Moon: Drawbacks in marriage. Partner may differ in age, social standing and financial position. Marriage threatened by death or disharmony.

Venus: Ambitious love nature. Restricted afflictions. Unhealthy and secret attachments which may upset the balance of mind. Intrigue with inferiors. Disappointments in love. Coldness and indifference of the partner. Marriage of convenience or for social position. Delay in marriage owing to difference in age, position or money or through parental position.

Mars: Early engagements with an inferior, social gain through marriage, which makes an important change in life and greatly affects later years.

Jupiter: Parents help or hinder the marriage. Domestic life greatly affects career.

Saturn: Opposed to marriage. Entangled in attachments with inferiors. Bad judgement in choice of partner.

Planets in Aquarius

Venus: May cause celibacy and platonic or romantic or secret attachments. Sudden beginning or ending of love affair. A love marriage, often after a long courtship. Trouble through difference in age of native and partner. May delay marriage to middle or old age.

Mars: Fortunate and happy marriage.

Jupiter: A love marriage to an older or elderly person.

Saturn: Faithful in love. A happy marriage or a pure romantic attachment and a lasting tie.

Planets in Pisces

Sun: For a woman, hindrance and obstacles in love affairs, financial gain by marriage but illness for husband.

Moon: Voluptuous and sexual nature. Numerous attachments before and after marriage.

Venus: Liable to detrimental entanglement. Delays, obstacles and secrecy in engagement and marriage. Partner may be an unworthy one, but marriage is likely to bring gain. May be followed by ill health. More than one union.

Mars: Disappointments in love affairs and delay in marriage. Two attachments.

Jupiter: Marriage to a social inferior. Obstacles to marriage arising out of scandal. More than one union.

Saturn: Handicapped by an unfortunate tie and a romantic attachment which ends tragically or sorrowfully. Unhappy marriage or an ailing partner. Trouble through servants after marriage.

5
Matching Horoscopes

The History of Matching Horoscopes

The institution of marriage has had a glorious past in India. Great thought had been bestowed on it: the Rishis of yore had envisaged as many as eight distinct features of marriage. These are:

1. Brahma,
2. Daivik,
3. Aarsh,
4. Prajapatya,
5. Asura,
6. Gandharva,
7. Raakshasa and
8. Paisacha.

The first consisted in giving the kanya (bride) to a well-behaved Vedic scholar. The second when the kanya was offered in marriage to the ritvik (priest) who presided over the father's yagna. In the third variety, the kanya was given in marriage to a groom in return for a couple of cows and oxen. Rishis could afford only that. In the fourth category, the young bride was given to a young groom to enable performance of household Dharma. It is claimed that children born out of such marriages are released of their sins besides enjoying excellent health and prosperity themselves. On the face of it, the above four types of marriage are no longer valid in today's context of our social, political and economic compulsions.

The fifth, Asuric variety, consists in a marriage between a boy and girl in which the expenditure goes beyond the parents' means. The children born out of this union will be wicked, habitual liars and engage themselves in disreputable activities.

The Gandharva type can be considered love marriage. They envisioned it for Kshatriyas as happened between Dushyanta and Shakuntala. No Dharma is said to be involved in this type.

The Raakshasa type of marriage is conniving as it is through force, violence and kidnapping. It may be illustrated by the Ravana type of marriages.

The worst in the list is the type that is contracted while the party is asleep, mentally deranged or by cheating, i.e., Paisacha.

It will be clear from the above description that the marriage of today can be labelled 'Asuric' and true to form, we inherit all kinds of problems. It certainly is not the Brahma type and cannot yield Dharma as dividend. But who cares?

A historical survey of the institution of marriage reveals that it was performed during the Vedic times on intrinsic merit alone and was oriented towards Dharma. There are no evidences of people comparing horoscopes for marriage nor was there the need for it. Even in Puranic times, we don't hear of it. Sri Rama had a horoscope and so did Sita, but neither Dasharatha nor Guru Vasishtha seemed to have asked for it. Sri Krishna had a horoscope, and we know that as Rishi Garga had made it, but Rukmimi's love letter rather than horoscopes seemed to have fixed the match. It was Gandharva-cum-Raakshasa with the consent of the bride, which is most important.

With the passage of time, however, values in life seem to have changed beyond recognition and the product known as merit seems to have evaporated. One had perforce to search for its nucleus, which they hoped to rescue from the horoscope at birth, and that is how horoscopes gained locus standing in the marriage market, with its good, bad and indifferent results. Having thus ruled the roost for some centuries now, it promises a queer dividend for the twenty-first century. It is this: matching horoscope for marriage should not be limited to the bride and groom alone; it should extend to the in-laws as well, to find out whether or not the mother-in-law will treat the daughter-in-law well, among other things.

It appears that for a long time, Koota examination has been the pièce de résistance in matching horoscopes for marriage. In this exercise, the target selected for examination has amazingly been the birth star or the Moon, which is the focal point of conduit of cosmic forces on man and his Chaitanya or consciousness, which speaks eloquently of the perception of the formulators of this Yuvaavastha or youth. All these Koota tools view this sensitive target from hundred angles through cameras, as it were, of differing powers and by feeding the result to the computer in our brain, churned out the verdict on the matchability.

Vaidyanatha in his *Mukurta Parijata* (unpublished) cites as many as 18 Kootas. These are:

1. Dina,
2. Gana,
3. Maahendra,
4. StriDeergha,
5. Yone,
6. Rasi,
7. Lords,
8. Vasya,
9. Nadi,
10. Rajju,
11. Linga,
12. Aaya,
13. Varna,
14. Vedha,
15. Yogini,
16. Paksh,
17. Gotra and
18. Bhoota.

Of their effects, he says:

> *One judges longevity from Dina; good health from Gana children; from Maahendra, conjugal happiness;*

> *through Yone, improvement of clan from Rasi; mutual attraction from Rasi Lord and Vasya; extreme well-being from Nadi and longevity of husband from Rajju.*

Without going into details about the mode of reckoning the different Koota, I shall content myself pointing to specific issues.

After mentioning the essential Kootas needed for the different Varnas, he declares: 'Friendship between the Rasi Lords, the Rases themselves, Nadi and Yone are specially advocated for all.'

He mentions that different Kootas are emphasized in different regions of the country and those Koota tests should be applied for those regions.

Vaidyanatha is an enthusiast of Amsa-Maitra and he says:

> *In the absence of friendship between Rasi Lords, should their Amsa Lords be friends, the former can be ignored. For matching marriage, friendship between Amsa Lords is the best, while their enmity should be avoided as far as possible.*

In the context of Dina Koota, he states categorically the name, and certainly not the nick name. Also, he countermands the same pada in the accepted same Nakshatras. In 6/8, he talks of Mitra Shashtashtaka, in which the bride happens to be odd Rasi, which is acceptable.

He countermands Eka Rajju (horizontal) and commends Bhinna Rajju; at the same time the mutual ascending/descending Rajju, but never compromises on the first by reason of the second.

Having said all this, Vaidyanatha emphasizes the need for consent in the marriage from the parties concerned before finalizing. He says:

> *The groom should first ascertain the consent of the bride, then ensure clearance of Dina Kootas. Having obtained them, he should subject the clearance to omens and only after obtaining it, must he wed the bride, thus fully satisfied on all counts.*

Vaidyanatha belongs to the fifteenth century, which appears to be the turning point in the history of marital astrology in India. For the first time, an astrologer in his person asks for the consent of the bride. In this respect, Kerala, as in all matters of astrology, appears to have spearheaded the movement and made matching horoscopes part and parcel of Muhurta (Electional) Astrology by inducting all the tools of Natal Astrology.

THE CHANGING CONCEPT OF MATCHING HOROSCOPES

Throughout the world, a radical change is taking place in the man–woman relationship and the institution of marriage is in jeopardy. At the same time, one also finds that family life is gradually falling apart. The group feeling fostered in the joint-family system, which extended to well-knit social relationships is disintegrating, even if it has not yet completely broken down. The impact of these changes on married life cannot be overlooked. The increasing rate of divorces and infidelity in conjugal relationships shows that a kind of distrust or wrong expectation from this human bondage has become rampant. Can we apply the traditional rules of married partnership taken from classical astrological treatises and feel assured that marriages will work out? One has to seriously study and consider these problems.

Ancient Indian society did not deny special importance to womanhood. It would be wrong to think that ancient Indians thought of womankind only in terms of their ability to bear children and propagate the race. The Vedantic philosophy postulated the same Divinity within women's bodies. According to it, it is not the form of an individual, whether male or female, but the consciousness within which decided the quality of the ego. There is no sex differentiation in consciousness, so the differences between a man and a woman who enter into marriage are not so vital, yet it is on the basis of this difference that marriages are solemnized.

Why should anyone marry? What do the partners expect from this relationship? Whose satisfaction or fulfillment would ensure happiness to them? What are the physical preparations necessary for securing minimal happiness in marriage? Is it companionship? Is it procreation and begetting offspring? Is it sensuous experience? What makes or breaks the foundation of marriage? Astrologers, especially Indian astrologers, claim that tallying of the partners' horoscopes could show to a great extent whether they would be happy with each other.

The Indian system of tallying the horoscopes has a very

rational basis. If one delves into the deeper aspects of the various classifications that are assigned at different points or numbers of comparability and total the same, one gets an overall picture of the agreement of two horoscopes. Presently, their essentials are lost and a kind of blind adherence to these numericals is observed. As a result, many astrologers have begun concluding that 50 per cent of the total points should be considered excellent. But unfortunately, it has come to notice that the high percentage of these points does not assure either psychological compatibility or harmonious relationship between the partners. Physical welfare of the two partners after marriage, the birth of children or such other welfare indicators of mutual benefit also cannot be assured on this basis. In many cases, in spite of a high degree of compatibility ratio on the basis of ancient texts, marriages have failed; the partners have either separated, divorced, died or lived in misery, bearing the ordeal of living together.

On the other hand, there have been marriages in which despite a very low degree of compatibility points, the partners have succeeded well in meeting the ordeals of living together in a more or less satisfactory manner. Evidently therefore, under the changed conditions of life, the ancient points of marriage compatibility require to be understood and applied in a radically different manner. We shall take up this discussion in a following chapter. Here, I wish to lay before the readers some other points which are important considerations in contemporary situations of life.

The first consideration, I would say, would be Lagna

compatibility. This is nothing new. Classical texts have already emphasized the desirability of such a consideration. The Ascendant in any horoscope is an indicator of the essential features of life as a whole. It represents the descent of life essence vibrating in the personality of the person during any specific incarnation. It shows the nature of his physical power, it shows the basic craving of his life, it shows the affinity of his life essence with other streams of such life currents. But in this connection, I wish to emphasize the planet ruling over the Ascendant sign, and the affinity of this planet with other planets. For example, if the Ascendant sign is Aries, Mars is the Lord of this sign. In such a situation, if the Ascendant Lord of the partner is Venus or Jupiter, the partnership could be very much like the combination in the charts. Even if the Ascendant is Scorpio, the same group of planets may be helpful. The rationale behind such grouping is the complementary nature of the physical characteristics of the planets and their moral and creative base. But this does not mean that for Sagittarius Ascendant, the compatibility preference would be the same as with Mars. One has to go deeper in the affinity of the Ascendant Lord with other planets at the physical and aspirational levels.

The second consideration relates to emotional compatibility. If the two people in marriage bondage are emotionally adjusted, the basis of the marriage is on surer ground. In this connection, one has to distinguish between emotional compatibility and emotionalism or infatuation. It is generally seen that in many cases when two people are emotionally attached to each other and are emotionally mature, their marriage proves successful. The 4th House and the Moon are concerned with emotions. Two sets of harmony are to be decided in the present context. The lord of the 4th House in both the horoscopes and the disposition of the Moon in them are important considerations. Though in astrological texts, the Moon is given more importance than the 4th House, yet it may be helpful to consider the contribution of the Moon in this regard. If the 4th lord is Mars in one case, with strong support from the Sun and Jupiter, while in the other case, it is Mercury with aspect from Saturn, the life of the two people will be spent in endless bickering and their emotional life of mutuality will come to an end as soon as the high tide of physical relationship is over. We have mentioned earlier that in marital happiness, the blending of consciousness is very important. In the given case here, as soon as the sexual desires are satiated, the consciousness would not fuse between them, rather they will drive each other away.

The third consideration relates to the nature creativity. In ancient societies, it was assumed that the birth of a baby cemented the relationship between the partners/parents. At that time, it was felt that procreation was a common means of mutual creativity. To a great extent, this assumption was right. But then, the children were produced as a desired goal; they were not an accident—unexpected, unwanted, or merely for the sake of social respectability, or to see the fulfilment of one's shortcomings and failures in life through the same fulfilled by the offspring. Children were respected as the arrival of Divinity for the salvation of the parents. Now, the situation has changed. Both the husband and the wife have different levels and aspirations of their creative channels. The birth of a baby is not necessarily on their desired list. Some may want to lead a sensuous life, be successful professionally or carve a name in the social circle, while there are others who want to contribute their special influence to society—be a poet, a painter, a writer, a social worker and so on and so forth. The incompatibility in this aspect of life is becoming an important feature of difference. The nature of creativity urges can be examined by studying the nature of the 5th House as well as the nature of the lord of the 5th House in both the charts.

The fourth factor relates to the consideration of the 7th House. There are many astrologers who attach the consideration of sexual relationship to the 7th House, but this is a very superficial view. A reference to any classical text would indicate that the 7th House is related to several aspects of one's life. The essential feature of this House is that it operates as the field, kshetra, for the activities of the 1st House, the inner core of the being. As the level of evolving egos rises, and matured souls are no longer tethered to physical and sensuous experiences for which the spouse was earlier considered the means, the deeper aspects of the 7th House must be examined. For example, the social life of an individual, business partnership and such other mutual intercourse with society at large in which context the expression of the personality of oneself is sought, are all related to the 7th House. But in case one person in the marriage partnership is attracted by social activities, wants to spend his time doing social work and welfare, while the other is interested only in one's hearth, drawing-room orgies and drinking parties, one can understand the degree of mutual relationship.

The fifth and the most important factor in marital happiness is the mutuality between the disposition of the 9th and 10th houses in both the charts. Every astrologer knows the importance of these houses in one's horoscope. If the nature of these houses in both the charts is not harmonious, the partners may live together and tolerate each other depending upon their planetary dispositions, but the necessary joy of living and evolving together would be absent.

Thus, for marital happiness, the important consideration is the possibility of the harmonious blending of the consciousness of two people as they grow together. Marital happiness depends upon the joy of living and growing together, meeting the ordeals of life together with courage and happiness and the sense of discovering the features of a larger life, which is not possible by taking into account the life of a single person, without opening the inner portals of one's consciousness to the other. This is an experiment in fusing the life of one into the life of the other. This process, once started, could teach the partners how to merge in the universal consciousness, which could, in turn, open the door to Divine Delight or Ananda.

SELECTING MARRIAGE PARTNERS

People approach astrologers when they have failed miserably in their attempts at solving personal and social problems. One approaches an astrologer if he/she has to be married or if he/she has a son, a daughter, a nephew or a niece to be married. An astrologer is able to help the client by giving them clues about the probable date of the wedding, the description of the bride or the groom, the direction from where he/she will come, how one's married life will be and so on. Notwithstanding anything contained in the ancient authorities and literature about marriage compatibility, there is no uniformity in any part of India with respect to comparing or matching horoscopes for the purpose of matrimonial alliances.

In North India, Koota and Manglik Dosha get undue importance and most other important factors are not even thought of, while in Tamil Nadu, Rajju and Manglik Dosha alone are considered to be very important. In Kerala, Papasamyam and Madhyama Rajju outweigh all other vital considerations. In other parts of India, too, some item or other of Dasa or Dwaadasa Koota get undue importance. Even today, there are orthodox people who consider properly matched marriages as less vulnerable to marital unhappiness. It is in this context that astrologers of the orthodox school are placed in an embarrassing position with regard to marriage matching.

Matching of horoscopes for matrimonial purposes assures lesser evil in married life. One can cross a busy road anywhere he likes, but when he crosses at zebra lines, the chances of accidents and death are limited. Similarly, a perfectly matched marriage leaves very little chance for marital unhappiness or even for dissolution. Horoscope matching is an art in itself and needs very skillful handling, backed by a fairly thorough knowledge of the rules, the exceptions and the provisions involved in this branch.

There are some apparent contradictions in Dasa or Dwaadasa Koota matching. For instance, Dina and Mahendra, Raasi and Vasyam, Dina and Vedha, Rajju and Yoni are but some examples. But each horoscope has to be considered in its entirety and not piecemeal and superficially. This would mean that an astrologer should first recast the two horoscopes (of the groom and the bride) to a uniform Ayanamsa that he follows. If an astrologer matches a Drik cast horoscope with Vakya cast horoscope or calculated on basically different Ayanamsas and declares them to match well or not matching perfectly, he will only be committing a blunder. Then he must consider to what extent the apparent contradiction affects the matching. For instance, Rasi Koota and Vasya Koota will negate Rasi Koota. Veda Koota will make Dina, Gana, Mahendra and Rasi Koota redundant in some cases. Nadi Koota is, of course, outside the compass of Dasa Koota, but its importance cannot be neglected under any circumstances. There are other items, too, such as Yoga Aanukoolya, Jaataka Aanukoolya, Dasa Sandhi and Dosha Saamya. An astrologer should not emphatically declare any two eligible horoscopes as perfectly matching or not matching at all unless he considers at length all important elements of Koota Shodhana and others.

The Vedas (Āpastamba Dharmasūtra) declare that marriage is performed 'for upholding Dharma and for begetting worthy children'. *Manusmriti* declares six types of regular marriages and two more which are either elective or forced. The arranged marriages of these days have been classified as Prajapatya type. There are restrictions with regard to boys or girls marrying blood relations, but Desachaara or customs prevailing in a region or among particular communities act contrary to these. But with the advancement of modern science and scientific temper, such blood-relation marriages are being discouraged, though only to a limited extent, because one cannot bring about change in the community or regional customs except over a period of decades. Notwithstanding anti-dowry acts and regulations, most of the arranged marriages in India are based on considerations other than astrological.

The shastras declare that while matching horoscopes for marriage, an astrologer should consider at least the following factors:

1. Koota Shodhana
2. Yoga Aanukoolya
3. Jaataka Aanukoolya
4. Dosha Saamya
5. Dasa Sandhi

As a prelude, they should invariably check the longevity of the bride and the groom, the general strength of the two horoscopes and all the mutual physical aspects. Koota

Shodhana invariably deals with Dwaadasa Koota, viz., Dina, Gana, Rasi, Yoni, Rajju, Mahendra, Vedha, Vasya, Graha Maitree, Deergha, Nadi and Varna. Each of these 12 items has got its own importance and therefore, every item has to be considered individually and in their totality. Then comes Yoga Anukoolya. The horoscope of the bride or of the groom should not be such that it cancels the benefic yogas and other aspects of the other horoscope; and the malefic yogas are to be kept at the minimum. Jaataka Aanukoolya takes care of marital bliss, sexual satisfaction, mutual adjustment, Putra Bhagya, fidelity, faith, physical health and other relations and above all, fortunes or misfortunes which cannot otherwise be detected. Therefore, this aspect needs particular consideration. Dasa Sandhi is very important as the effect of that will either cause or cancel misfortunes.

In this book, it is proposed to deal with Dosha Saamya or cancellation of naturally malefic aspects or neutralization of humours. In a female horoscope, the significance of the 12 Bhavas, in addition to what are normally perceived in male horoscopes are as given below, according to Devaakeraleeyam.

The shastras say that while comparing horoscopes for marriage, an astrologer should consider the following procedure:

Kanyaayaah Purushasya cha Prathamato Nirneeyamaayuh Punaha
SantaaNadi Tatetaram cha Sakalam Daivagna Varya Sthataa.

Bhaaviprasna Vilagnatopi Nikhilam Paanigraham Kaarayat
Santaanaaya Yatah Prayaati Nitaram Preetim Pitroonaam Ganah.

—Prasna Samgraham

It means that while matching horoscopes, an astrologer should first determine the longevity of the bride and the groom. If this is satisfactory, then he should next examine from the horoscopes if they (the couple) will be blessed with children, health and wealth including Dharmic rites. Thereafter, that astrologer should set up a prasana and cross-check the marriage compatibility. If both horoscopes are matching and prasana is fully satisfactory, then alone the marriage should be settled/performed

Coming to Dosha Saamya, the shastra says:

Dampatyoraikyakaale Vyaya, Dhana, Hibuke, Saptame, Klagna, Randhre

Lagnaat, Chandraasche Sukraat Ahi, Ravi, Ravijaa, Bhommi Putrah, Dwayoscha Tatsaamya, Putra Mitra Prakara, Dhanayutam Damptee Deerghakaalam Tapintekatra Heene Mrutiriti Munayaha Praahuratryadi Mukhyaahaa.

It means while matching horoscopes for marriage, an astrologer should examine in both the bride's and groom's horoscopes the position of Rahu, Sun, Saturn and Mars in relation to the 12th House, the 2nd House, the 4th House, the 7th house Ascendant and the 8th House and find out whether there is proper compatibility or cancellation of dosha, whether such compatibility assures good progeny, long life, good relations and happiness. If one of the two horoscopes lags behind, then there will be death or incompatibility. This is the opinion handed by rishis such as Atri, Bhrigu, Kautsa, Vashishtha, Gautama, Kashyapa and Angirasa.

RESEARCH INTO MARITAL HAPPINESS

When the world was young and evolution of animals into human beings was taking place and a portion of humanity had not yet lost its inheritance of tail, there lived a fully developed and sublime man, Sri Rama, king of Ayodhya. The epic, Ramayana, goes to say that he was great in all respects, but he lacked marital happiness. He was first deprived of his consort by force and at a later time by public opinion, leading to eternal separation for the rest of his life. Every Indian knows Rama's story, and fortunately, the great man's horoscope is preserved, which shows that he was a Cancer man with a Mars in bad House.

Coming to our modern times, we find that Jawaharlal Nehru, who, while attaining greatness in all respects, lost his partner in the prime of life and was denied marital happiness. He was also born under the influence of Cancer. Even some of my relations, natives of Cancer, were denied marital happiness, even though they were all placed in happy circumstances otherwise.

These facts have given rise to an idea in my mind

that while Cancer is capable of producing great men, it has consistently ruined their wedded lives, and therefore, I make a general survey of Cancer Ascendant with particular reference to Mars and marital happiness.

CHARACTER

People having Cancer as their Ascendant are weak if the Moon is near Amavasaya. There are chances of the Moon becoming isolated (Kemadruma Yoga) and eclipsed by Rahu (Grahana Yoga). These situations bring weakness and disaster to the native. Mercury is the lord of the 12th and 3rd houses, which shows expenditure on brother and sister, but lack of happiness and satisfaction from them. The Sun being the lord of the 2nd, combination of Mercury and Sun does not pay much, as it means combination for deposits and expenses. The natives are honest, sincere and truthful, as Jupiter is lord of the 9th House. They control their feelings and value spiritual elevation and company. Venus being lord of the 4th and 11th houses, there are good chances of earning wealth, building houses, acquiring properties and buying vehicles. Generally, if Venus is eclipsed by the Sun, these chances are not fully available. Their mothers, too, (in case of eclipsed Venus) suffer a lot in their life. The 6th House lord being Jupiter, they create enemies by their lenience and want to adjust with them. Jupiter being a half benefic for them, their religious pursuits and fortunes are generally imperfect and enemies and obstacles come in the way. If Jupiter, Venus and Mars are well placed, they are very lucky and happy. Mars is completely benefic for them. They generally get a long life especially when Mars or Sun aspects the 8th House, but their death is sudden. The 10th lord being Mars, they are very successful in their profession and the combination of Mars and Jupiter creates good results. They are temperamentally honest and religious due to the predominance of the Moon as Ascendant lord and Jupiter as lord of the 8th House. Due to lordship of Saturn on 7th and 8th houses, they might have an unhappy domestic life and marry more than once or may have a plurality of wives. They are industrious and frugal, but are often miserable. Being extremely sensitive in distress, they feel nervous easily, especially when the Ascendant is aspected by a malefic planet or the Moon has weak conjunctions. They are self-reliant and like fair play. They have a good reputation as traders and industrialists. The Sun does not inflict death. Venus, Mercury and Saturn are evil and unfriendly to the Cancer Ascendant and bring death.

6
Some Yogas

A few important yogas arise for Cancer natives; of course they depend on planetary positions. Some of them are as follows:

1. If the Moon is situated in the Ascendant along with Jupiter and Mars, the native is deeply religious,
2. If the Sun and also the lord of the 7th and 10th houses are strong, the native acquires ruling powers,
3. If the Moon and Mars are in debilitation, the native is a villain, even if he is the foremost among the learned,
4. If the son of the Moon, i.e., Mercury, is in 5th House and is afflicted by malefic association or aspect, it gives wealth in its Dasa or ruling period,
5. If a strong Moon is posted in the 11th House, the native undoubtedly attains his cherished goal in life, and
6. If Saturn and Mars are together in the 11th House, the native marries a girl who is in love with him.

If Venus is in Aries and Mars in Taurus, this exchange

between the lords of 10th and 11th houses constitutes a Maha Yoga, for which very good effects are attributed. Again, Venus is the ruler of the 4th and the 11th. Rulership of the 4th makes him a yoga-karaka, but that of the 11th is evil for all planets. However, if Mars is in Aquarius and Saturn in Aries, the exchange is between the rulers of the 8th and 10th houses. It is an evil one, known as Dainya Yoga. If Jupiter is in the 8th and Saturn is in the 9th, it is also the same yoga causing ups and downs in life. On the other hand, Saturn in Sagittarius, Jupiter in Capricorn and Venus in Libra, the resultant yoga is the exchange between rulers of the 7th and 9th houses, forming a Maha Yoga, which is considered equal to a Raja Yoga. Yet another important yoga arises with Mercury in the 6th, Jupiter in the 7th and Venus in the 8th houses. It can also arise when Sun and Mercury are in the 6th, Mars and Venus in the 7th and Jupiter in the 8th. But Mercury should not combust. However, this latter yoga is not considered as good as the former. There is another Raja Yoga if the lords of the 5th and the 7th exchange places.

THE 7th HOUSE

For Cancer, Capricorn is the 7th House. In this case, the marriage partner will be practical, tactful and reserved. Progress in career and parental influence appear to weigh in, concluding an alliance. Separation is unavoidable due to some hindrance. Reserved mentality and mutual suspicion break harmony. If Saturn, however, receives good aspect, then the marriage partner may be adjustable. If he receives only bad aspect, then the partner is thrown into sickness and melancholy. If Saturn is posited in Cancer, the marriage partner is said to affect the health and personal matters of the native in the absence of beneficial aspects to the House.

Mars is the yoga-karaka for Cancer because he owns the 5th (triangle) and 10th (square) houses. But the question arises, whether or not for the Cancer born, if Mars is posted in Capricorn, there is Kuja Dosha. But there is no such dosha since Mars is a yoga-karaka occupying the house of exaltation. On the other hand, Ruchaka Yoga, one of the Mahapurusha yogas, is formed with Mars in the 7th for Cancer Ascendants. The rule is that Mars is very powerful if he is in Kendra, which happens to be his own House or House of exaltation. Its effects are that the native will possess strength, fame and fine qualities. He will be well-versed in sacred hymns, praying, the art of producing malefic spells and science. He will become a king or a king's compeer. He will have an attractive personality, be liberal, victorious and wealthy, and will live for 70 years in comfort. The yoga endures for life and the effect will be felt more during Kuja Dosha and his Bhukti.

Regarding marriage alliances for Cancer, some people opine that Leo and Aquarius, and Capricorn are exceptions to the rule of samasapthama, which is considered to be par excellence. There are other important factors that are responsible for unconventional unions, extramarital affairs or disharmony in married life. A few illustrations are given below.

Females

In a woman's horoscope, the Sun in Gemini will bring two love affairs or marriages. The Sun afflicted by Uranus indicates elopement, seduction or prevents marriage. If, at the same time, Mars afflicts the Moon or Venus, seduction is seriously threatened. When the Sun is afflicted by Uranus, she is liable to go astray and form an illicit union with a married man, and she leaves the husband especially when the 7th is occupied by Neptune or Mars.

The Sun in conjunction or affliction with Mars makes the person highly passionate and if in good aspect to Jupiter, she will play the harlot with servants and inferiors. If Venus is strong, it will be with men of superior birth.

Any aspect of Saturn or its conjunction or parallel to Venus in particular and generally to Sun and Mars prevents the immoral conduct by delays, hindrances, obstacles and lack of opportunity.

If the ascendant falls in between 5 degree-0' and 10 degree-0' Aries, Gemini, Leo, Libra, Sagittarius and Aquarius or 20'-0' to 25'-0' Taurus, Cancer, Virgo, Scorpio, Capricorn, and Pisces, the native is likely to turn out a harlot, while the ascendant in between 5'-0' and 12'-0' Taurus, Cancer, Virgo, Scorpio, Capricorn and Pisces and in between 25'-0' and 30'-0' of Aries, Gemini, Leo, Libra, Sagittarius and Aquarius makes her oversexed.

At the time of birth, if Venus is occupying the degrees of 13'-20' to 160'-40' Capricorn, or 0'-0' to 3'-20' or 23'-20' to 260'-40' of Aquarius and Saturn is posited in between

0'-0' and 6'-40' Taurus or 10'-0' to 16'-40' Libra, while the two planets aspect each other fully, the woman goes all out to satisfy her desires.

Uncontrollable yearning in women is indicated by their ascendants falling in 3'-20' to 6'-40' Taurus or 13'-20' to 16'-40' Libra.

She, as well as her mother, will be a loose woman, whose ascendant falls in a sign of Mars of Saturn, where Venus is posited in association with the Moon and aspected by strong malefics.

The 12th House coinciding with Aries or Scorpio where Rahu is posited in combination with a strong malefic is a sure sign of adultery. The 7th falling in Cancer occupied by Mars and the Sun in combination is an unmistakable indication of the native's low morals. Such a woman will have no husband, but many affairs. The combination of Mars, Venus and the Moon in the 7th House renders her uncontrollably passionate. When both the ascendant and the Moon are closely hemmed in between strong malefics and are wholly devoid of aspects or associations of benefics, a woman will have undesirable men. Adulterous affairs are indicated by the combination of Mars with a malefic in the ascendant or in the 4th, 7th, 8th and 12th houses.

Occupation of the 8th from the ascendant by Mars and Rahu is conducive to perversions in women. Women, whose Saturn and Mars are in the 5th from the ascendant without any association or aspect of benefics, will conceive before marriage.

The position of the lord of the 9th in the 6th, 8th or

12th shows strong preferences for men of low status.

In case the ascendant and the Moon are in odd signs, such ladies will have manly features, with an evil nature. In Libra, while the two planets aspect each other fully, it makes the woman go all out to satisfy her desire. When Mars is the ruler, Venus is in it or when Venus is the ascendant, the women will have loving disposition and be faithful to her husband. Venus in sextile to Mars in a woman's map indicates easy access to her in courtship. If Mars and Venus be in feminine signs, she will love and take delight in men's kindness.

When Mars rises in Taurus, Libra or Capricorn, the native will be immodest and unchaste. When the Moon and Venus are posited in the ascendant, the woman becomes short-tempered and pleasure-seeking. If a malefic is posited in the 5th House, which should be its debilitation sign and is fully aspected by an inimical planet, the subject turns an immoral woman of a base nature.

For girls born in Pisces ascendant, if Mars is in the 8th and Venus occupies the House of Mars or Saturn or associates with them, the girl becomes immoral. Jupiter's aspect will definitely mitigate the Martine evil as he is a benefic. If Venus is posited in a sign of Mars and Mars in a sign of Venus, the woman will take paramours and prefer them to her husband. While Venus and Mars are thus posited, if the Moon and the Sun occupy the 7th House, the woman will have intercourse with other men with the consent of her own husband. If the 3rd lord, being a natural malefic, joins the Rahu anywhere, she will have many illicit connections, overpowering her husband. If the 5th lord, being a natural malefic, joins the Rahu in the 3rd, the woman will quarrel with her husband and go astray. She will have plenty of lovers and many would be ruined on account of her.

She lives by prostitution in whose chart the cruel lord of the 9th is posited in the 10th in close combination with Rahu or Ketu. The combination of the lord of the 9th with Saturn or Rahu in the 10th shows that such women will not even mind public places. Malefics in the ascendant or the 7th House, when their lords fall in the signs of malefic planets, the native will be immoral. Lord of the ascendant and the lord of the sign occupied by the Moon are hemmed in between malefics and entirely devoid of all benefic connections, the native will be immoral.

Aries or Scorpio coinciding with the 12th or the 8th House, where Rahu is posited with another malefic, the woman will be immoral. Mars and the Sun in 7th House, in any sign, renders her uncontrollably passionate. The results will be more prominent if Cancer is the sign in 7th House.

Affairs with many men are shown if Venus is posited in between 0'-0' and 3'-20' and 23'-20' and 26'-40' Aries, Leo and Sagittarius; 10'-0' to 13'-20' Taurus, Virgo and Capricorn; 3'-20' to 6'-40' or 20'-0' to 23'-20' Gemini, Libra and Aquarius; 13'-20' to 16'-40' Cancer, Scorpio, Pisces and Mars is placed in between 3'-20' and 6'-40' or 20'-0' and 23'-20' Aries, Leo and Sagittarius; 13'-20' to 16'-40' Taurus, Virgo and Capricorn, 0'-0' to 3'-20' or 23'-20' to 26'-40' Gemini, Libra and Aquarius or 10'-0' to 13'-20' Cancer, Scorpio and Pisces.

A very weak malefic in the 7th aspected by benefics will make the woman unchaste. The Moon and Venus with malefic aspects occupying the ascendant in Aries, Scorpio, Capricorn or Aquarius, the women becomes unchaste and pleasure-seeking. A malefic ascendant with a malefic posited therein, when two malefics combine in the 6th House, the native will be immodest and unchaste.

Ascendant/Moon in the first five degree (0'-0' to 5'-0') of Aries, Cancer, Virgo, Libra or 5'-0' to 10'-0' of Leo, Aquarius; 5'-0' to 12'-0' Capricorn; 18'-25' Aquarius ; 20'-0' to 25'-0' Capricorn, last five degree of (25'-0' to 30'-0') Aries, Taurus, Gemini, Leo and Scorpio, increases the woman's libido and she goes all out to quench her desire.

Adulterous affairs are indicated by the combination of the lord of the 9th with Rahu in the 12th or 10th House. A malefic lord of the 9th strengthens the effect.

The Sun in a double-bodied sign, and malefics afflicting the sign signify more than one marriage or union. A second marriage is a must if at the same time fruitful signs occupy the 1st, 5th or 7th House.

Males

The Moon and the Saturn in the 7th House, the man will be of immoral nature. The 7th House with all malefic connections, the native will be of immoral nature. Mercury in the 7th House coinciding with his debilitation or inimical sign, the native chooses vagrant women for sexual appeasement. Venus posited in the 7th House identical to Aries, Scorpio, Capricorn or Aquarius and aspected by Mars or Saturn, the native will have no moral code or constancy.

Mars and Saturn occupying the 7th House identical to Aries, Scorpio, Capricorn or Aquarius signs, the native will be of immoral nature. The Moon in the 7th or the 12th House posited in malefic sign (Aries, Scorpio, Capricorn, Aquarius), when Venus is afflicted by malefics, the native will be of immoral nature.

Rahu and the Sun in the 7th House will make the native lose all his wealth through his fornications. The lord of the 7th House in the ascendant and when lords of the 6th and 2nd houses combine in the 6th House associated with malefics, the native will be of immoral character. The association of the 7th lord with Rahu/Ketu aspected or conjoined by Mars or Saturn when Venus is unpleasantly posited, the native will be of immoral nature.

The combination of Jupiter and Mercury or the Moon and Venus posited in the 7th House or aspecting it when the 7th House is very strong, the native will have intercourse with innumerable women. Saturn with Rahu or Ketu in the 7th House from the ascendant makes the native approach immature girls for his amatory needs.

The Moon posited in the 7th gives pleasure to the native only with the females of the lower strata of society, with Mars in the 7th, takes women during their periods. The man with the Sun in the 7th of his horoscope takes barren women, while the one with Venus or Jupiter in the 7th, finds pleasure with pregnant women.

Lord of the ascendant, the 2nd and the 6th houses posited together in the 7th House in association with the malefic, the native will have many wives or be an adulterer and seek women other than his wife.

If Venus is in the 7th House with Rahu or Ketu and has the aspect of, or association of a malefic or is in a movable sign, with Rahu or Ketu, the person will be a profligate. If the 7th House be afflicted together by aspect or conjunction of Saturn and Mars, and lords of the 1st and 6th are conjoined, the native will be an adulterer. Venus in Aries, Taurus or Aquarius gives the native many women. Saturn aspected by Mars posited in the 7th in Aries or Scorpio makes the native take women of all classes.

Lords of the 5th and 7th houses associated with malefics and having connections of the lord of the 6th House, the man will be of immoral nature. Venus aspected by Mars and posited in the sign Aries or Scorpio and devoid of the aspect of Jupiter, the native will be of immoral nature. The Moon and Venus aspected by malefics in the ascendant identical to Capricorn, Aquarius, Scorpio or Aries, the native will be of immoral nature. Venus and Mercury in the 7th, the 8th or the 10th House or Venus and Mars in the 7th or in the 10th, the native will be of immoral nature. Lords of the 6th and the 7th in the 2nd in combination with a malefic, the native will be of immoral nature.

If Mercury, Venus and Saturn be in the 7th or 10th, identical with Libra or Taurus, the native will be a profligate. The native will be blindly sexual when the lords of the 6th and 7th are in the 9th in association with a malefic. A debilitated malefic in the 5th House aspected by an inimical planet, the man will be of immoral nature. Malefics in the ascendant, the 12th and the 7th and a weak Moon in the 5th, the man will be of immoral nature. The association of Saturn and Mars in the said House when the 1st, 4th, 5th, 7th, 9th and 10th are occupied by strong malefics, makes the man behave in an immoral manner. It adds to the force when the combination of Saturn and Mars occur in the 1st, 4th, 5th, 7th, 9th and 10th.

The combination of the strong lords of the 7th and 11th or their mutual aspect or their occupation of 1st, 5th or 9th houses, makes the native immoral. Lords of the ascendant and the 6th House falling in the rising sign in combination with a malefic makes the native immoral. Lord of the ascendant and of the 6th in combination with malefics and aspected by malefics induce the man to commit indiscriminate adultery. Lord of the 2nd, 6th and 7th houses in ascendant, or Venus associated with a malefic in the rising sign or the lord of the 7th House combined with a malefic posited in the ascendant, all these show the immoral nature of the man, and the native will be an adulterer. The lords of the 2nd and 12th houses posited in the 3rd House and aspected by Jupiter or by the lord of the 9th House, the native will be of immoral character.

If a malefic is posited in the 1st or 7th, he will have illicit connections with other women; women will voluntarily join him, if Venus is in the 7th or 11th with the Moon. Libra being the ascendant, Rahu or Ketu in the 7th, Venus in Scorpio, with the Moon and Mars in the 11th, the native will have a union or marriage out of the common. Sagittarius as the rising sign, with Mars in the 9th, and Mercury and Venus in the 12th, the native will be an adulterer.

The man in whose horoscope Saturn is aspected by Venus in Aries or Scorpio or associated with the lord of sex, is blind with lust and will not flinch to perpetrate anything. Saturn and lord of the 7th occupying the 2nd from the ascendant in association with the malefics, the native will be an adulterer.

The union of the lords of the 2nd, 7th and 10th in the 10th house, the person born will have illicit relations with women other than his wife.

The lord of the 9th falls in the 7th while the lord of the 7th is in the 4th. Also the lords of the 10th and 11th uniting in a square induce the man to commit indiscriminate adultery. Venus in the 10th House from the Moon or Saturn in the 10th House from Venus or Venus in his own sign or Venus in 10th or Mercury and Saturn in the 10th House, the native will be addicted to more than one woman. The Moon or Venus in association with malefics posited in the 1st, 4th, 7th or 10th House and aspected by malefic planets make the person highly passionate.

It is impossible to define what all things a man will do to quench his sexual needs when the lord of the 10th House is aspected by Saturn or when the 10th lord is posited in Aries or Scorpio fully aspected by Venus. The exaltation of the lord of the 7th, his occupation of a friendly sign or his own position in his signs or his combination with lord of the 10th in square or trine.

The Sun or the Moon posited in the 4th House with association and aspects of malefic planets or the 4th House getting connection of strong malefics. The lord of the 4th House have associations with and aspects of malefic planets without any benefic touch whatsoever when the lord of the 7th is stronger than the lord of the ascendant.

The actions of the man in whose horoscope Mars is in the 4th from the ascendant and Rahu, Sun and Saturn are in the 7th in one and the same sign will be indescribably vulgar.

The man in whose chart Saturn is posited in the 7th and Mars in the ascendant will attract even old women, and the man in whose horoscope all the squares are occupied by strong malefics unassociated and unaspected by any benefic will indulge in unnatural acts. Rahu or the Sun in the 7th and Mars in the 4th or 7th shows the native's animal aptitude. The lord of the 7th posited in the 4th when the lord of the ascendant is in the ascendant, the 7th or the 2nd, the native will be an adulterer.

Venus in the ascendant without any benefic connection when posited in between 16'-40' and 20'-0' Aries, Leo, Sagittarius; 26'-40' to 30'-0' Taurus, Virgo, Capricorn or 6'-40' to 10'-0' Cancer, Scorpio, Pisces, prompts the native to molest girls. In this combination, if Venus is in the ascendant in association with malefics or aspected by them, the native runs after women in public.

Libra being the ascendant with Mars, Moon, Rahu, or Ketu in the 7th, the native will be an adulterer. Taurus rising with Moon, Saturn, and Venus in ascendant, the native will be an adulterer. If the lord of the 7th along with Venus occupy a malefic sign, the native will be lustfully inclined.

The combination of a weak Moon with a malefic in the 7th while the lord of the 7th is associated with a malefic in the ascendant, the native will be lustfully inclined.

Venus occupying a dual sign whose lord is in exaltation while the lord of the 7th is powerful, the native will be of immoral nature. Venus in Virgo or Cancer aspected by Saturn makes the native prefer low women.

The native whose Venus is posited in Gemini or Virgo and fully aspected by Mars will be always troubled by sexual desire. He may waste all his possessions for his pleasure. Venus in Leo aspected by Mercury gives the same result.

Venus and Mars in the 7th House and the Venus is placed in between 0'-0' and 3'-20' or 93'-20' and 26'-40' Aries, Leo, Sagittarius; 10'-0' to 13'-20' Taurus, Virgo, Capricorn or 3'-20' to 6'-40' or 20'-0' to 23'-20' Gemini, Libra, Aquarius or 130-20' to 160-40' Cancer, Scorpio, Pisces and Mars is posited in between 3'-20' to 6'-40' or 20'-0' to 23'-20' Aries, Leo, Sagittarius or 13'-20' to 16'-40' Taurus, Virgo, Capricorn or 0"-0' to 30-20' or 23"-90' to 260-40' Gemini, Libra, Aquarius or 10'-0' to 13'-20' Cancer, Scorpio, Capricorn. He will be so mad with urge that he will do anything with women. In whose chart the lord of the 7th occupies Aries or Scorpio in combination with or aspected by Venus, the same result can be unhesitatingly asserted.

Venus in Aquarius ascendant in between 25'-0' and 27'-30' Aries, 22'-30' to 25'-0' Taurus, 20'-0' to 22-30' Gemini, 170'-30' to 20'-0' Cancer, 15'-0' to 17'-30' Leo, 12'-30' to 15'-0' Virgo, 10'-0' to 12'-30' Libra, 7'-30' to 10'-0' Scorpio, 5'-0' to 7'-30' Sagittarius, 2'-30' to 5'-0 Capricorn, 0'-0' to 2'-30' Aquarius, 27'-30' to 30'-0' Pisces and Saturn in opposition to Venus, the above results will predominate.

Any aspect of Uranus to the Moon in male chart inclines the man for an illicit contact with the married women. Instead of the Moon, if it is Venus, the illicit cohabitation will generally be with the unmarried or single woman; however much the females dislikes him, they are attracted to him if Venus is afflicted by Uranus. Should the Sun be afflicted by Uranus or any other malefics in a male chart, he will suffer heavy misfortune and bad health, the conjunction of Venus and Uranus is not good on moral plane, and the House involved will be chiefly affected.

Any aspect of Saturn or its conjunction or parallel to Venus in particular (and generally the Moon and Venus in a male nativity) prevents the immoral conduct by delays, hindrances, obstacles and lack of opportunity. If Mercury, Venus and Saturn be in the 10th or a House identical with a sign owned by Venus, the person concerned will become a profligate.

VIVAHA MUHURTA

Ancient sages have laid great emphasis on the selection of Vivaha Lagna because it affects the quality of married life, profession, profits, etc.

According to Saint Vashishtha, lagna may fall in any sign provided that sign is associated with or aspected by a benefic planet. But he mentions only four Navamsas, viz., Gemini,

Virgo, Libra and Sagittarius (first half) for marriage. Thus, the period in each Vivaha Lagna has been restricted. There is one more restriction on Navamsa; it should not be the last Navamsa unless it is Vargottama, which is considered very auspicious, indicating good progeny and fortune in life.

Of the four Navamsas mentioned above, Libra is not the last Navamsa in any sign. Gemini Navamsa is the last Navamsa in the signs of Gemini, Libra and Aquarius. It is in Gemini sign that it becomes Vargottama and is good for Vivaha Lagna. Virgo is the last Navamsa in the sign of Taurus, Virgo and Capricorn, so it becomes Vargottama in Virgo sign. Sagittarius is the last Navamsa in the sign of Aries, Leo and Sagittarius. So it becomes Vargottama in Sagittarius sign. Thus, we see that Vargottama Navamsa as the last Navamsa fall in dual sign of Gemini, Virgo, Sagittarius and Pisces. On this basis, only 30 Navamsas in 12 signs qualify for performance of marriage ceremony. Vivaha Muhurta requires fortification of the 7th House. In view of this, the 7th House must not be occupied by any planet. In order to strengthen Vivaha Lagna and the Moon, placement of some planet in specific houses is desirable. For this, the Sun, Rahu, Ketu and Saturn should be in the 3rd, 6th or 11th House. The Moon should not be in the 1st, 6th, 8th or 12th House. Mercury can be in any House except the 8th or 12th. Jupiter and Venus should be in the 5th, 9th 10th or 11th House. Venus should not be in the 3rd House, according to sage Vashishtha.

Varahamihira mentions Gemini, Virgo and Libra as ascendants for marriage and Navamsas of these signs in other ascendants. In order to strengthen Vivaha Lagna, he has suggested that malefics should occupy the 2nd, 3rd or 11th House, benefics should occupy places other than the 7th, 8th and 12th of this ascendant. Venus should not be in the 6th and Mars in the 8th House. The Moon should not be associated with the Sun, Mars, Venus or Saturn and should not be in between two malefics.

In Muhurta Ganapati, an effort has been made to synthesize the views of Vashishtha and Varahamihira and give a mathematical formula to determine the strength of Vivaha Lagna. The formula is named as Vimsopaka Bala. Each planet occupying the desired House is allotted some units of strength and the total of these units is 20 (Vimsha). If planets get more than 10 units in any Vivaha Muhurta, it is considered strong and that Lagna is recommended for marriage ceremony. This is explained below.

Combustion of Jupiter and Venus

In fixing the time of the wedding, we have to see that Jupiter and Venus do not combust. Marriages are prohibited when the Moon, Jupiter or Venus is combust. The Moon is combust every month and this combustion has been discussed under this for marriage. A planet before combustion is termed as Vriddh (old) and on rising after combustion, it is known as Bala (infant). Marriages are also prohibited during periods of Vriddh and Bala Avasthas of both Jupiter and Venus. While all agree that the period of combustion is to be avoided in toto, opinions differs on the period of these two Avasthas. This period ranges from three to 10 days.

The Role of Stars

Tara Bala: The constellation ruling at the time of birth is one's Janma Nakshatra or birth star. Count from the birth star to the one ruling on the marriage day and divide the number by 9, if divisible. Otherwise, keep it as it is. If the remainder is 7, it is termed as Naidhana and indicates danger. It should be avoided while fixing the day of the wedding.

Chandra Bala: The zodiacal sign in which the Moon is situated at the time of one's birth is one's Janma Rasi or Birth Moon. The Moon at the time of the wedding should be in a favourable sign from Janma Rasi. All signs excepting the 4th and 8th from Janma Rasi are considered good. This is applicable to both bride and bridegroom.

Guru Bala (Strength of Jupiter): This is considered for girls only. If on the day of the wedding, Jupiter transits a sign which happens to be the 2nd, 5th, 7th, 9th and 11th from her Janam Rasi, it is considered 'good'. If he happens to transit the 4th, 5th or 12th sign from her Janma Rasi, it is termed 'bad'. If he transits, the 1st, 3rd, 6th or 10th sign from her Janma Rasi, it is termed as 'Pooja', which indicates that marriage can be performed after performing remedial measures for Jupiter. When Jupiter is termed as 'bad' but transiting his sign (Cancer), marriage can also be performed after doing double or treble Pooja, depending on the sign when counted from Janma Rasi.

Surya Bala (Sun's strength): This is considered for boys only. If on the day of the wedding, the Sun transits a sign which happens to be 3rd, 6th, 10th or 11th from his Janma Rasi, it is considered good; if in 4th, 8th or 12th sign, it is considered bad, if in 2nd, 5th and 9th sign, it is considered Pooja (to be worshipped), and in 1st and 7th signs, special Pooja is to be done. No marriage can be performed when the Sun is 'bad'. In two Pooja categories, therefore, it can be done after doing prescribed Surya Shanti.

Panch Banas or Panchaka (Five-Source Energy)

According to Dr B.V. Raman,

> *Five sources of planetary stellar and zodiacal energies are involved. Take the number of lunar day (from the lst of the month—bright halt), the number of the week day (Sunday, Monday, etc.) the number of the constellation (from Aswini) and the number of the Lagna (from Aries). Add these together and divide the total by 9. If the remainder is 1 (Mrityu), it indicates danger; if 2 (agni) risk from fire; if 4 (raja), bad results; if 6 (Chora), evil happenings and if 8 (roga), disease.*

In marriage and Upanayanam, Roga and Mrityu Panchaka should be avoided. These can be divided into two categories, viz, major evils and minor evils. Major evils are to be avoided throughout the universe, whereas minor evils are to be avoided in specified regions only.

Panchanga Dosha: We have already discussed these under lunar day, weekday, constellation, yoga and karma. Bad items mentioned there fall under Panchanga Dosha.

Ravi Sankramana (Solar Ingress): When the Sun is about to leave one sign and enter another, such times are not recommended for any good work. Sixteen Ghatis (six hours 24 minutes)—both before and after the entry of the Sun into a new sign—should be rejected while selecting a muhurta for wedding. For solar ingresses into Aries, Cancer, Taurus and Capricorn, the time limit is three days instead of 16 Ghatis.

We should reject 32 Ghatis for solar ingress (16 before and 16 after), 2 Ghatis for the Moon, nine for Mars and two for Mercury.

Sagraha Chandra Dosha: The Moon's association with any planets should be avoided. This association acts like poison. The Moon if associated with the sun gives poverty; with Mars, death; with Mercury, no issues; with Jupiter, ill luck; with Venus, desertion by wife and with Saturn, an ascetic life.

The Moon's association with Mercury or Jupiter is accepted as good or beneficial by some sages, and these are mentioned in *Vasishtha Samhita*.

Kartari Dosha: When two malefic planets are situated on either side of the Lagna, i.e., in the 12th and 2nd houses and the planet in the 12th House is in direct motion and the planet in the 2nd is in retrograde motion, it is known as Kartari Dosha. If both the Lagna and the Moon are in between malefics, the bride dies.

Exceptions: The Moon in 6th, 8th and 12th houses in a marriage Lagna should be avoided. The Moon should not be in the Shadvargas of malefics.

Kujasthama Dosha: Mars should be avoided in the 8th House because it kills both the bride and the bridegroom.

Bhrigu Shataka: Venus should be avoided in the 6th House of a marriage chart because it leads to separation and the bride may go to the extent of killing her husband.

Gandantham: This is of three types, viz., Nakshatra, Lunar Day and Lagna Gandanta. The last two Ghatis of Ashlekha, Jyestha and Revati and the first two Ghatis of Makha, Moola and Aswini should be rejected for marriage. The last two Ghatis of the 5th, 10th and 15th (Full Moon) and the first two Ghatis of 6th, 11th and 1st (Dark-half) Lunar days should be rejected for marriage. Similarly, the last two degrees of Cancer, Scorpio and Pisces and the first two degrees of Leo, Sagittarius and Aries should be rejected.

Ekaraala Dosha: This evil falls when the marriage constellation counted from the constellation in which the Sun is situated is an odd number (including Abhijit) and the yoga of the day is one of nine yogas declared bad (Vyatipata, Vaidhruti, Parigh, Gand, Atiganda, Shoola, Vyaghata, Vajra and Vishakumbba).

Vara Dosha: Sage Vashishtha mentions (Yama Ghantaka) and (Kulika) as evils. In *Muhurta Martanda*, we find their method to determine their exact time on different days. There are 15 muhurtas in a day. If we divide the diurnal duration by 15, we get the exact time of each muhurta. The 14th Muhurta on Friday, 12th on Saturday, 10th on Sunday, 8th on Monday, 6th on Tuesday, 4th on Wednesday and the

2nd on Thursday is termed as Yama Ghantaka.

The 14th Muhurta on Sunday, 12th on Monday, 10th on Tuesday, 8th on Wednesday, 6th on Thursday, 4th on Friday and 2nd on Saturday is termed as Kulika. Both these are rejected in daytime only as per dictum.

Visha Ghati Dosha: Four Ghatis (1 hour 36 minutes) of each constellation are termed as Visha Ghati (poisonous period), therefore to be rejected in marriage. Even the ascendant rising at the time of marriage may fall in these Visha Ghatis and should be rejected. Sage Vashishtha says the period of four Ghatis is to be counted from the time when the constellation is past the number of Ghatis indicated in brackets as follows:

Aswini (50), Bharani (24), Kritika (30), Rohini (40), Mrigsira (14), Aridra (21), Punarvasu (30), Pushya (20), Ashlekha (32), Makha (30), Poorva Phalguni (20), Uttara Phalguni (18), Hasta (21), Chitra (20), Swati (14), Vishakha (14), Anuradha (10), Jyestha (14), Moola (56), Poorvashadha (24), Uttara Shada (20), Sravana (10), Dhanishtlia (10), Shatbhisa (18), Poorva Bbadrapada (16), Uttara Bhadrapada (24) and Revati (30).

If a marriage is performed in Visha Ghati, the girl is widowed within three years.

Ashtama Lagna/Rashi Dosha: The Lagna ascending at the time of marriage should not happen to be the 8th from the Janma Lagna of the bride and bridegroom. It should also not be the 8h from the Janma Rashi of the bride and bridegroom. The Lord of the 8th from the Janma Lagna and the planets situated in the 8th from the Janma Lagna of both the bride and bridegroom should also be considered. The signs owned by these planets should not be the ascendant and Navamsa rising at the time of marriage.

Exception: If the lords of Janma Rashi and the 8th Rasis are friends or the same planet is the lord of both, this dosha is nullified as per the dictum.

Akala Vrishti Dosha: When there is rainfall out of season, the day is deemed unfit for marriage.

Kumuhurtha: A sidereal day consists of 30 muhurtas: 15 diurnal and 15 nocturnal. Of these, some are considered bad. The bad diurnal muhurtas are the 1st, 2nd, 4th, 10th, 12th and 15th. In nocturnal muhurtas, the 1st, 2nd, 6th and 7th are bad.

Mahapatha Dosha: This happens when the Sun and the Moon are equally removed from the equator on the same side of it. It is also termed as Kranti Samya (Equal Declination) and is calculated according to mathematical formulae beyond the scope of this book.

Vaidhruthi Dosha: An evil yoga formed by the Sun and the Moon.

Lagnast Shuddhi (Lagna and the 7th house): Lagna stands for the self and the 7th for the wife. Both these should be strong. The Lagna should be occupied or aspected by its lord, a friendly planet or a benefic planet. The Navamsa Lagna should he similarly aspected by or associated with its lord, friendly or benefic planet. Similarly, the 7th House, its lord and Navamsa Lagna should be favourably disposed.

It means that if the Navamsa Lagna of the rising ascendant at the time of marriage is not aspected by or associated with its lord, it kills the bridegroom. Similarly, the Navamsa Lagna of the 7th House if not associated with the bride. If both the Navamsa Lagnas are associated with their respective lords, friends or benefics, the couple is blessed with sons and grandsons.

Grahana Bham Dosha: If the eclipse is full, seven days are to be avoided on either side of date of eclipse. If it is partial, three days only and the same period if the Sun or the Moon sets in under eclipse, the Nakshatra, in which an eclipse appears to be rejected for six months for marriage.

Krura Viddham Dosha: The constellation having a Vedha from a malefic planet is considered as afflicted and rejected for marriage purposes.

Krura Samyzutta Dosha: The constellation occupied by the Sun at a given moment and the one immediately preceding and succeeding it have to be rejected for purpose of marriage.

Utpata Bham Dosha: Chapter 21 of *Vashishtha Samhita* deals with Upagrahas. Here, we count from the solar constellation to the Vivaha Nakshatra. If this happens to be 14th, it is termed as Patha; if it is 15th or 19th, it is termed as Ulkapatha and both are rejected for marriage purposes. These major evils can be countered by strong good combinations in the Vivaha Lagna.

Some of the important combinations from *Vashistha Samhita* are as follows:

- Jupiter, Mercury or Venus in the ascendant
- Jupiter in Lagna has the power to destroy all evils due to Lagna, Navamsa, malefic aspects, etc.
- A planet occupying ascendant which happens to be his Moola Trikona sign/own sign and aspected by benefics or friends. This is true in case of friend's sign and Navamsa
- Any planet situated in Lagna, and 4th and 10th houses in his exalted sign/Navamsa aspected by benefics or friends
- A Vargottama planet is situated in the ascendant or aspects it
- If the lord of the ascendant is in his own Navamsa, exalted Navamsa or in the Navamsa of Adhi Mitra, Mitra (friend) or benefics
- A benefic lord of the ascendant situated in 1st, 3rd, 4th, 5th, 6th, 9th, 10th or 11th House
- A malefic lord of the ascendant situated in 3rd, 6th or 11th House with Sthana Balam (positional strength, one of the six kinds of strength)
- Benefic planets situated in 1st, 4th, 8th, 9th, 10th or 11th houses
- Powerful benefic situated in the 2nd House. Here, the word 'powerful' means 'strong' in Shadabala. Powerful Sun and the Moon destroy evils arising on account of Ekargala, Upagraha, Patha, Latta, Tamitra, Kartari and Udyasta.

A few special combinations have been mentioned as follows:

Mahendra yoga: Jupiter in the ascendant; Venus in the 8th and the Sun in the 11th make this yoga. If Mercury is not combust, this yoga brings happiness of all kinds.

Vishnu Priya yoga: Venus in the ascendant; Jupiter in the 10th and the Sun and Mercury in the 11th make this yoga.

Ardha Nari yoga: Venus in the ascendant; Jupiter in the 11th and 8th houses vacant make this yoga.

Shreenatha yoga: Venus in the 2nd; Jupiter in the 12th, Sun in the 8th and Saturn in the 6th make this yoga. This yoga confers happiness and wealth.

Samundra yoga: Venus in Lagna, Jupiter in the 4th, Mercury in the 2nd and Saturn in the 11th make this yoga.

Maha Vishnu yoga: Mars in the 3rd, Saturn in the 6th, Venus in the 9th and Jupiter in the 10th constitute this yoga.

Pushya yoga: Saturn in the 3rd, Jupiter in the 6th, the Sun in the 10th and Mars in the 12th constitute this yoga. This yoga gives happiness in many respects.

Sthairya yoga: Strong Jupiter with Venus in Lagna constitutes this yoga.

Jaya yoga: Venus with Jupiter in Lagna exalted or otherwise strong. Both the planets should be strong in Shadabala. This yoga confers luxury and property.

Vijaya yoga: Mercury, Jupiter and Venus are all strong and in Lagna constitute this yoga. So far we have discussed the theoretical side of Vivaha Muhurta. It is very difficult to find a flawless Muhurta. We should select a time which has more good points and less evils. We should select a time when the Sun, the Moon, Jupiter, lord of the ascendant rising at the time of marriage and the lord of Lagna, Navamsa, are powerful.

7
How To Perform a Wedding Ceremony

In India, especially among Hindus, a wedding ceremony is considered a pure and beautiful bondage of two souls approved by seven rotation of the heavenly fire, Agni. The newly-weds are blessed so that they live harmoniously and happily throughout the whole life making adjustments as and when needed. But alas! It is shameful on our part that we do not care for the importance of the chosen period for this ceremony as has been given to us by the great rishis of yesteryears. We see that while matching horoscopes of the bride and bridegroom, we go to the astrologer to ask the time of the tilak ceremony, a symbolic conception ceremony (Godh Bharai) and at last, the most important selection of Lagna of marriage for seven rounds of the Agni by means of doing a yagna (havan). Yagna Karta Pundit must be learned in the Vedas, the Puranas, etc.

First of all, the bridegroom's party should engage the bride in Uttrashada, Swati. Sravana, Poorva Bhadrapada, Poorvashada, Poorya Phalguna, Anuradha, Dhanishtha, Kritya or in the Nakshatras of marriage which are Rohini,

Mrigasira, Magha, Uttraphalguna, Hasta, Swati, Anuradha, Moola, Uttrashada, Uttra Bhadrapada, Revati. The tithi should be all except 4, 9, 14 and 30 leaving aside Bhadradi Doshas. The days should be Monday, Wednesday, Thursday, Friday. There should not be Veda in Nakshatra. According to Electional Astrology, the fixed time or Muhurta should not be neglected. Nowadays, modern Hindus think this cultural function as superstition. The selected Muhurta is ignored and the wedding ceremony is not celebrated at the fixed time, which results in widowhood, family conflicts, sickness, divorce, no children, etc., and astrologers are unfairly blamed.

Who is responsible for this? No doubt we are. We knowingly neglect our culture and try to emulate the West. The wedding ceremony should be solemnized while the Sun is in Aries, Taurus, Gemini, Scorpio, Capricorn and Aquarius signs. At the time of marriage, the position of the Sun should be 3, 6, 10, 11 from the birth sign of the bride. When the Sun is in 1, 2, 5, 7, 9 from the birth sign of bride, it is called Red Worship, or worshipping the Sun. This should only be allowed in emergencies. Only for a person born in the Libra sign, Sun worship is not bad, as they are married only after worshipping the Sun.

The Jupiter of the bridegroom should be 2, 5, 7, 9, 11 from her birth sign in transit and when Jupiter is in 1, 3, 6, 10 from the birth sign of the bridegroom, it is called Yellow Worship or worshipping Jupiter. The Sun and Jupiter from their birth signs as well as the Moon should not be 4, 8, 12 at the time of the wedding. The Moon should be 1, 2,

3, 5, 6, 7, 9, 10, 11 from the birth signs of both the bride and bridegroom.

If the son or daughter is the first issue/first-born, then the birth month, birth Nakshatra and birth tithi should be omitted. In the same way, for the first issue, either the bride's or bridegroom's jyestha month should be omitted because three jyeshthas (bride-bridegroom month) is called Trikhala Dosha, which is harmful to both parties.

In a household, within six months of the son's marriage, the daughter should not be married. When marriage is settled and if any death occurs on either side of the bride or the groom within three *peedhis*, e.g. grandfather grandmother, maternal gandfather, maternal grandmother, then in emergency, the marriage ceremony may be celebrated after a month.

Horoscope Matching

In horoscope matching, a few pointers need to be kept in mind. The varna of the girl should not be superior to that of the boy. In two different Nakshatras, when the same Yoni is indicated, it should be committed, as they are mutual enemies. When both have the same Gaiia, it is very good and facilitates in increasing love. Raakshasa and Manushaya result in death and Raakshasa and Devgana in struggle and should be omitted. 6-8 signs are death giver, 5-9 signs are harmful to pregnancy, 2-12 signs give poverty hence these should be omitted and only 6-8 signs are allowed when their lords are friends. This is called Preeti Khadastaka.

When lords of both signs are friends Gana Dosha is cancelled. When both are born in the same Nadi, it is not admissible. If both have Madhaya Nadi, death is certain. Hence, it should be cancelled. Nadi Dosha is cancelled when the birth Nakshatra is the same but Charan are different. From ancient times, it is said that Nadi Dosha for Brahmins, Varna Dosha for Kshatriyas, Gana Dosha for Vaishyas, Yoni Dosha for Shudras is admissible. Hence, for four Varnas, this should also be considered well. In Guna's matching, 19 to 27 are medium and more than 27 are very good.

Nakshatras of both should not be 1, 3, 5, 7 to each other. There are three groups of Nakshatras. If the bride's and bridegroom's Nakshatra fall in the same group, that is very auspicious. These three groups are as follows:

1st group: Revati, Ashwini, Bharni, Kritika, Rohini, Mrigsira.

2nd group: Aridra, Punarvasu, Pushya, Ashleslia, Magha Poorva Phalguna, Uttraphalguna, Hasta, Chitra, Swati and Visliaklia.

3rd group: Anuradha, Jyestha, Moola Poorvashada, Utrashada, Sravana, Dhanishta, Shatbhisha, Poorva Bhadrapada; Uttra Bhadrapada.

When the bride and the bridegroom are of the 1st group, the bridegroom is dear to the bride. When both are of the 2nd group, they love each other naturally. When they are of the 3rd group, the bride is dear to the bridegroom.

Listed here are a few aspects that should be avoided:

Gandanta Dosha: The last 48 Ghatis of Jyeshtha, Revti, Asheslia should be omitted. This is called Nakshatra Gandata Dosha. The last 12 minutes of Cancer, Scorpio, Pisces ascendants and the starting 12 minutes of Aries, Leo, Sagittarius should be omitted. This is called Lagna Gandata Dosha. The last 24 minutes of Poorna tithis 5, 10, 15, starting 24 minutes of Nanda tithis 1, 6, 11 should be omitted. Thus, these three Gandanta Doshas are inauspicious and to be omitted.

Kartari Dosha: Malefics directional in 12th House and retrograded in 2nd House is Papa Kartari Yoga, which brings death, poverty and melancholy and hence, to be omitted.

The combination of Moon with Mercury and Jupiter is good.

From birth Lagna or Moon sign, the marriage muhurta is decided. Only when there is friendship between their lords, is the 8th sign allowed.

According to astrological texts, the following are called Visha Ghatis, which are to be omitted in marriage Lagna: 30 to 34 Ghatis of Revti, Magha Nakshatra, 40 to 44 Ghatis of Rohini, 18 to 22 Ghatis of Uttraphalgulna, 20 to 24 Ghatis of Uttrashada, 14 to 18 Ghatis of Mrigsira and Swati, 24 to 28 Ghatis of Uttrashada, 21 to 25 Ghatis of Hasta, 10 to 14 Ghatis of Anuradha, 56 to 60 Ghatis of Moola.

Nakshatra Vedha according to Panchshaluka chakra and Saptashalaka Chakra should be omitted.

Libra, Scorpio, Sagittarius are deaf in the day after

midday. Capricorn is deaf at night. Aries, Taurus and Leo are blind in the day. Gemini, Cancer and Virgo are blind at night. Aquarius in day and Pisces at night are dumb. Capricorn, Aquarius and Pisces are lame during sunrise and sunset. If there is deaf Lagna at the time of marriage, then it brings poverty.

If day-blind, then widowhood; if night-blind, then death of progeny; if lame Lagna, then loss of wealth. If these malefic Lagnas are aspected by their lords, then they are beneficial. Hence, while deciding Vivaha Lagna, the above-mentioned points should be considered.

If marriage takes place in Navamsa of Sagittarius, Pisces, Gemini, Virgo or Libra, the girl will be equal to Sati or Pativrata.

Last Navamsa should be omitted. Only Vargottama Navamsa is admissible.

Saturn in the 12th, Mars in the 10th, Venus in the 3rd and the Moon in any malefic House and Venus, Moon in the 6th or 8th should not be considered auspicious.

Godhuli Vela is the best for marriage Lagna, but there are some rules for Godhuli Vela. Here are the Godhuli Velas: in cooler days, i.e. in November, January and February at sunset time when the sun seems round, it is Godhuli on Thursday after sunset and on Saturday sun in the sky is good Godhuli.

Moon in 1, 6, 8 kill the bride, Moon in 1, 7, 8 kills the bridegroom, Moon in 1,2,3, is very good.

Pata, Vyatipat, Dagdha tithi, combustion of Moon, Venus and Jupiter, Tithi Kshaya, Tithi Vridhi, Bhadra,

Sankranti, Lala Vedha, Yama, Upgraha doshas should well be considered. So that the life of the new couple may be healthy, wealthy and happy throughout with long life.

Mars in 1, 4, 7, 8, 12 produces Kuja Dosha and the horoscope is called Manglik. Both of the horoscopes should be Manglik for the Kuja Dosha to be cancelled.

Why Time Is Important

Timing an event is certainly an important, interesting but intricate part of astrology. Marriage is an important milestone in one's life which thoroughly changes the course of the life of a native. Timing this important event correctly is definitely rewarding for the astrologer and satisfying for the querist. But in spite of the research work of stalwarts in astrology, the question is yet to see its master solution. Having worked on this problem for a number of years, I feel that there is no method that is foolproof. The planetary indications are to be studied and applied quite intelligently to derive successful and accurate results.

Divorce is a painful situation, but we cannot turn our face from this ground reality with respect to some unfortunate native. 'Hope for the best and prepare for the worst' is an old dictum. Prior knowledge of this unforeseen happening and its time surely helps one to at least prepare for the worst. I am giving these observations from my experience. Let's first discuss the timing of marriage.

Determine, Denial or Delay

Before embarking upon finding the period of marriage, it is imperative to find out whether the native is destined to marry at all. If yes, try simply to judge if it would take place between 18–28 years of age or thereafter. Generally, the affliction by Saturn and undesirable position of retrograde planets delay marriage.

The reasons for delay in brief are:

1. Lords of the 7th and the 2nd occupying Saturn's sign or receiving the adverse aspect of Saturn.
2. The luminaries and Karka Venus under the influence of Saturn being in his constellation, sign or Navamsa.
3. Influence of retrograde planets on the 2nd or 7th or their lords by ownership, occupancy or aspect.
4. Affliction to the 2nd or 7th House and planets in fixed signs or Navamsa.
5. Conjunction or mutual aspect between Saturn-Mars, Venus-Moon, Venus-Sun, Sun-Saturn, provided the involvement of the 7th House is there in one way or the other.
6. If the distance between the Sun and Venus is 43' 20', Venus is debilitated and aspected by Saturn, the marriage is delayed.

It is good to remember that Mars obstructs the marriage upon 28 years, Saturn upon 31 years and Saturn-Rahu upon the age of 36 years.

Mark the Major Period

Having judged delay or otherwise, and even if one is not able to judge the approximate span, we should look into the planets whose major period is running between 18 to 35 year. If the Dasa of one or more planets operates within this period, one is to carefully mark the planet that is a strong significator of the concerned House. Our study reveals that marriage mostly takes place in the Dasa Bhukti of Rahu if this Dasa comes during marriageable age.

Select the Sub-period (Antardasha)

Selection of one sub-period out of nine, in the Dasa marked as above, is a comparatively difficult task, as there may be more than one planet indicating marriage. Following may be used as a guidance to select the particular Bhukti or Antar Dasa.

Note the lords, as well as occupants, of the 4th and 9th houses in addition to those of the 2nd and 7th. Find which among them is the most powerful. The Navamsa should also be considered to decide the same like the Lagna or Rasi chart. It may be kept in mind that marriage can take place in the Dasa Bhukti of yoga-karaka planets and also such as Mars for Cancer and Leo Ascendants, Venus for Capricorn and Aquarius Ascendant and Saturn for Taurus and Libra Ascendants.

The sub-period of the Moon and Venus can also bring marriage. As hinted above, the 9th House does play a very important and significant role in marriage timing, Marriage can take place in the Dasa Bhukti of significator of the 9th House, especially if they are to 2nd or 7th House. It would be useful to note that Sade-Sati of Saturn does not obstruct marriage, if other indications are satisfied.

Time through Transit

Transits modify timing. Transits of Jupiter and Saturn should be considered, after finding out the probable sub-period to further narrow the time of marriage. Transit of Jupiter should promote either the 2nd or 7th House, either by aspect or by passing through them. Jupiter's transit in the 6th and 8th House is equally important as that will affect the 2nd House. As such, Jupiter should transit either through Lagna 2, 3, 6,7, 8 houses during the probable sub-period, to bring about marriage. Jupiter's transit through 5th and 9th houses is also important, as this promotes Lagna.

If Jupiter passes through the 7th House and crosses the Navamsa position obtained by the 7th lord or Venus, the marriage may take place.

Similarly, the transit of Saturn should influence the 5th or 7th House at the same time when Jupiter's transit will be promoting marriage probabilities.

Jupiter's transit thus would indicate a period of about one year, which can further be reduced by taking the common period of transit of Jupiter which is covered under the subperiod of the planet giving marriage.

Pick Pratyantar for Preciseness

The Pratyantar Dasa (subperiod) may be picked correctly by taking the help of Lagna and Navamsa charts. The Pratyantar Dasa lord should influence the Lagna or the 7th House as far as Navamsa chart is concerned. Thus find out the most common period of all, which will be the probable time of marriage.

There may be more than one planet whose sub-sub period may seem to bring marriage and in that case, the transit of fast-moving planets may help. Consider the transits of 7th lord, Venus and the Sun. It is not essentially so, but in a number of cases, I have found that the transit of the Sun in the sign of sub-sub period lord brings marriage. Transit of Venus in the sign of Bhakti lord may also be taken into consideration.

A consideration of the country, circumstances and the period must also be made before forming any judgement. If we work on a birth chart step by step, we will have amazing success in our observation of timing of marriage.

8
Issues in a Marriage

A number of research observations have been made over the time of marriage, but practically no work has been done in determining divorce and its duration. I will make an honest attempt to find out whether divorce will take place in a marriage. If so, when will it be evident?

Various combinations have been laid down in different texts to determine the conditions for divorce, but it is difficult to remember all such combinations. We will, therefore, try to confine ourselves to the basic fundamentals only.

Basic Principles Tending Separation

1. The Sun, Rahu and Saturn are the planets which are associated with separative tendency. The dispositor of these planets also carries the same effect but to a lesser degree. The 12th House governs separation. The 12th lord also has a tendency towards separation.

    The divorce will not take place in spite of very critical relations between the couple. In case of Cancer Ascendant, Rahu is in the 7th, the 7th lord Saturn occupies the 4th in opposition to Mars and Sun who are conjoined in the 10th. The separation was quite likely, but that could never happen, by the grace of God, due to the 4th lord of Venus in the 9th House in exaltation sign and Jupiter.

2. The planet who possesses separative effect and damages, the planets causing marriage, will bring divorce in its period.

3. Separation takes place during the sub-period of the planet which forms the combination for divorce but brings marriage. This is most unfortunate. In such Dasa, marriage must be avoided to check probabilities of separation immediately after marriage.

4. The separation may also result during the sub-period of the planet which spoils the 4th House, particularly if that planet owns the 6th, 8th or the 12th House. In addition to this, the planet also contains the separative tendency by nature or ownership.

5. The misfortune of getting separated may come during the sub-period of the Sun, Saturn and Rahu if these are in the 4th, 7th or 12th, forming the combination of separation.

6. The 6th lord may also bring about divorce if that is placed under the separative effects in the 2nd, 4th, 7th or 12th House.

7. For Libra Asendant, if Mars and Mercury join the 12th and 14th lord, Saturn falls in the 6th, the divorce will come in Dasa Bhukti of either of these planets.

8. The marriage, if it takes place during the Dasa of the

afflicted 2nd lord, then divorce will take place in the period of the planet afflicting the 2nd lord.

9. In certain cases, we have to see the position of malefics from Venus or the 7th lord. If malefics are there in the 6th, 8th or 12th from Venus, divorce takes place. If the 4th afflicted is also malefic, divorce is unavoidable. In such a case, the adversity will be also attached to the date of marriage.

Chart 1: Born 4.1.1957 at 2h. 46m. (IST) at 27 N 32, 80 E 43 with a balance of 5 years 4 months 7 days of Mars Dasa at birth

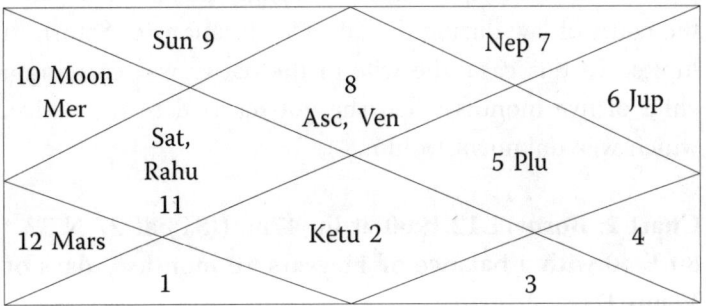

Two Divorces

The marriage of the native (Chart 1) took place on 17.06.1980 during Jupiter-Jupiter period and divorce took place on 30.10.84 during Jupiter-Saturn period. Second marriage was solemnized on 22.02.85. Jupiter in the 9th in debilitation caused marriage. The 12th lord Mars and Saturn both have afflicted Jupiter. Therefore, the same major period caused divorce. Saturn who contains separative tendency, has afflicted the 7th House in Rasi and Navamsa charts as it falls in the 7th House under Vargottama Navamsa in Scorpio. Rahu and the 6th lord Venus are also associated with Saturn in the 7th. Therefore, it was the sub-period of Saturn which brought divorce through court. The 4th lord Sun occupies the 6th under debilitation and Mars aspects the Sun. Here, the Moon is a malefic. The 4th and the 4th lord Sun are both under Papakartari Yoga. Thus, the 4th House has been damaged and comes under the influence of separative Yogas. The 7th House and Venus also come under the heavy influence of separative planets. Thus, in the present birth chart, divorce is strongly indicated through the court of law during the adverse vibrations of Saturn in Jupiter. In this case, the wife of the native was carrying a child of five months when she got married to the native, which was unknown to him.

Chart 2: Born 11.12.1960 at 1h. 47m. (IST) at 27 N 32, 80 E 40 with a balance of 11 years 10 months 7 days of Venus Dasa at birth

8 Sun, Mer	Nep 7	5 Plu, Moon, Rahu	4
	6 Asc		
	9 Jup, Sat	5 Plu	
10 Venus	12		2
	11 Ketu	1	

The Loss of Chastity

The native of Chart 2 belongs to a royal family of Rajas whose marriage (of 2.04.90) ended in a divorce in her 31st year on 28.04.90 during Rahu Jupiter period. Legal divorce was granted during Rahu-Saturn period. I have said in the earlier part that the 4th House has great importance in timing marriage and deciding divorce. Jupiter in the 4th in own sign caused marriage in the major period of Rahu. Most of the marriage takes place in Rahu Dasa. Here, Rahu is 5th from Venus and Mars is 6th, whereas the Saturn and Jupiter are 12th. Thus, 6th, 8th and 12th houses from Venus are occupied by malefics having separative effects and the lord of the 4th and 7th Mars and 8th House from Venus. Saturn in the 4th with 4th lord Jupiter under mutual aspect with Mars is a strong indication of separation, as discussed earlier. Even if we look at the case from the position of 7th lord Mars, we find that Mars possesses separative effect and joins the 7th under mutual aspect with Saturn and Jupiter. The 7th lord Mercury falls in the 12th with the separative are present for Lagna, from the Karka and the 2nd lord Venus and also from the 7th lord Jupiter. The Navamsa position of the 7th and the 4th lord Jupiter in Leo and the 9th lord Sun in Aquarius. Saturn in Scorpio has further spoiled and denied conjugal happiness. Therefore, the native being the daughter of the family of a Raja, was blamed for the loss of her chastity and left by her husband on the very first day of her meeting with him.

Chart 3: Born 16.2.1948 at 23 h. 27m. (IST) at 78 E 11 29 N 23. Rasi Ascendant 19411 1 0; Sun 30311 5 1; Moon 1711 52; Mars (R) 125,19; Mercury (R) 31011 39; Jupiter 24011 52; Venus 3421,48; Saturn (R) 11 511 29; Rahu (R) Lahiri's 250 9; and Ketu (R) 20511 9 with a balance of 13 years 2 months 8 days of Venus Dasa at birth.

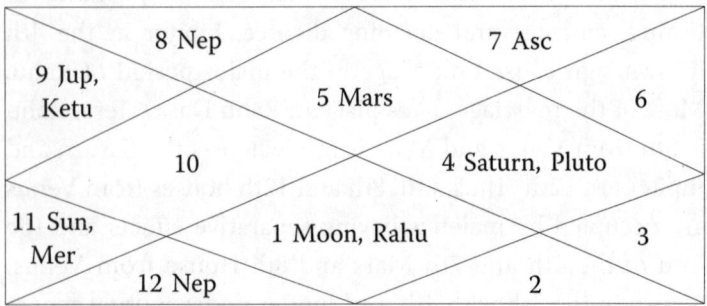

Home spoiled

Marriage (Chart 3) on 13.06.69 during Moon-Rahu period, divorce on 10.12-.84 after 15 years of marriage due to dowry. The Moon and Rahu are in the 7th and brought marriage during that period. Mercury is the lord of the 12th and Mars is the 7th lord placed in the 11th in retrograde motion. Thus, mutual aspect of the 7th lord Mars and the 12th lord Mercury, both planets retrograde is adverse for the continuation of marital life. The 4th lord Saturn is also retrograde in the 10th and aspects the 4th. Therefore, 4th is not spoiled much. That is the reason that separation took place after 15 years of marriage. The Lagna lord Venus is exalted in the 6th and is hemmed between inimical Sun and Moon. This is always bad if Venus is either conjoined by either of the luminaries or hemmed between them. If Venus falls in Cancer or Leo and the Moon in Gemini or Virgo or Cancer and the Sun on the other side of Venus, conjugal and the Sun on the other side of Venus, conjugal bliss will be curtailed, There are malefics in the 6th, 8th and 12th from Venus. The 7th lord Mars obtains the Navamsa of Venus and in Navamsa chart, the 7th lord Sun is under the influence of Rahu, Mars and Saturn. The separation came in evidence during Rahu-Saturn period as both have spoiled the matters of the 7th House. Saturn is 4th lord from major period lord Rahu and that spoiled the home for the native.

Chart 4: Born 14.10.1960 at 17hr 10m. (IST) at 28 N 27, 78 E 49 Rasi Ascendant 3461, 26, Sun 177" 48; Moon 10711; Mars 7711 19; Mercury 302. 27; Jupiter 244047; Venus 20711 51; Saturn 25911 10, Rahu (R) Lahiri's 140,16; and Ketu (R) 320,16 with a balance of 16 years 6 months 19 days of Mercury Dasa at birth

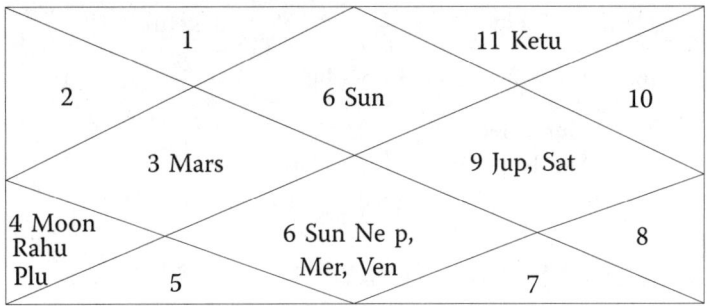

Unfortunate Marriage

The native of Chart 4 got married on 09.02.1987 during Venus Dasa Bhukti. The Sun is the 6th lord and is in the 7th Mars and the 12th lord Saturn aspects the 7th and the Sun is there. This indication is sufficient to foresee separation, but the examination of the 4th House will further strengthen our observation. The 4th lord Mercury, who is also the lord of the 7th, is in the 8th with 8th lord Venus. In addition to this, the 4th House is tenanted by the 2nd lord Mars in inimical sign under mutual aspect with 12th lord Saturn. These factors are enough for granting divorce soon after marriage.

Chart 5: Born 5.11.1954 at 23h. 50m. (IST) at 126 N 51, 80 E 56. Rasi: Ascendant 11311 1; Sun 1991 34; Moon 3121,56 Mars 2860 52; Mercury (R) 18611 24; Jupiter 960 29; Venus (R) 21411 22; Saturn 1981,56; Rahu (R) Lahiri's 9550 9; and Ketu (R) 7511 9 with a balance of 9 years 6 months 9 days Rahu Dasa at birth

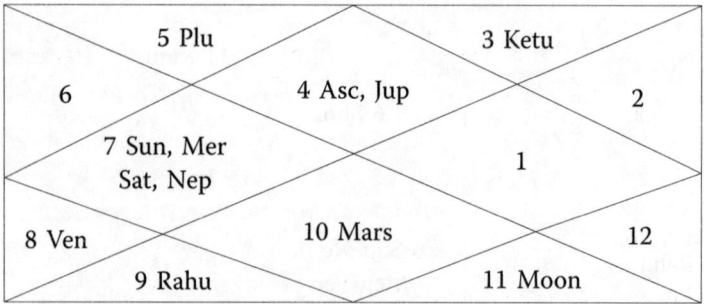

The Sun obtains Vargottama Navamsa and is associated with Saturn in Navamsa aspected by Saturn in Rasi chart and such an afflicted Sun is the 12th from Dasa lord Venus. Therefore, it will be the sub-period of the Sun which will finally separate the native from her husband which was running from 03.09.87 to 03.09.88. The sub-period of Saturn brought about the misfortune.

Separation

In Chart 5 of a charming female, there are three exalted planets in quadrants: Jupiter, Saturn and Mars. She is the daughter of a very famous and successful physician. She had been a brilliant scholar throughout. It was a most unfortunate incident in her life that she fell in love with a boy from another caste during her college days and married him on 28.02.75 in spite of great opposition from her parents, during the Jupiter Moon period. She was blessed with a girl child after three years on 02.05.78 and separated from her husband in early 1980 during the Saturn period. The Lagna is weak as its lord falls in the 8th. Therefore, the exaltation of the three most important planets and many Raja Yogas even could not bring a happy and prosperous life. Parents of the native have strong faith in astrology. No astrologer predicted the tragedy of her divorce. On the contrary, they predicted a very prosperous life as the yoga-karaka Mars is exalted in the 7th and the 9th lord is exalted in the Lagna. In fact, the 7th and 8th lord Saturn in the 4th with the 12th lord Mercury and 2nd lord Sun is responsible for separation. The 12th lord Mercury, 8th lord Saturn and the 2nd lord

Sun, all possess separative influence most distinctly. The lord of the 4th Venus, who falls in Martian sign Scorpio in the 5th is placed in between malefic like Saturn and Rahu. That spoiled her sweet home.

The 4th House has been damaged maximum by Saturn, therefore the separation took place during the Saturn period. The separation may result during the Das Bhukti of planets who spoil the 4th, particularly if it owns the 6th, 8th or 12th and also possesses separative tendency. In the present case, Saturn has the maximum effect of separation as it spoils the 2nd lord Sun, by nature and ownership of the 8th and also the significator Venus.

Chart 6: Born 29.3.1959; Sun 3450 10; Moon 32311 2; Mars 4311 57; Mercury 35411 3; Jupiter (R) 1520 7; Venus 34 10 1; Saturn (R) 23 1" 1; Rahu (R) Lahiri's 2080 46; and Ketu (R) 2811 46 with a balance of 12 years 4 months 3 days of Jupiter Das at birth

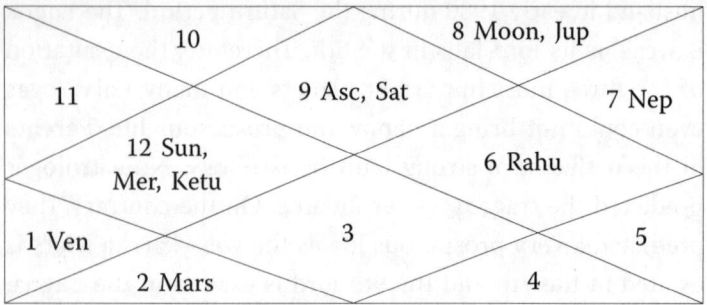

Late Marriage and Immediate Divorce

The lady (Chart 6) had a late marriage at 32 years and sought divorce practically just 10 days later due to torture by her husband. The marriage took place on 27.01.89 during Mercury period running from 2.8.88 to 29.12.90.

The 12th lord Moon who joins the 7th in Saturn's sign is mainly responsible for divorce. The 4th House is also damaged as the lord of the 6th Saturn fall occupies it in retrograde motion. The opposition of Saturn and Mars in the 4th House is always adverse for a sweet home. Mercury owns the 11th and 2nd houses and is in the sign of debility in the 8th in association with the Lagna lord Sun and the dispositor of Rahu, Venus. There is mutual exchange between the 2nd and 8th lords, Mercury and Jupiter. In Navamsa, the Sun is in the 7th in mutual aspect with Mars. Mercury is in the Navamsa of Saturn. Marriage took place immediately after the commencement of Mercury Dasa and the affliction of Mercury resulted in divorce immediately thereafter. Legal divorce was granted in November 1991 during the sub-period of Ketu in Mercury.

Separation is a wide subject and needs exhaustive study to find the cause of it. A question arises whether separation can be avoided, particularly if that is shown in the birth chart. I believe that can be managed, provided we seek the help of an expert astrologer while selecting the match. In a number of cases, strong possibility of separation has been neutralized to an appreciable extent seeking the help of an astrologer and by matching of horoscopes. The selection of time of marriage may also be of great use. Marriage should be avoided during the Dasa of a planet indicating marriage and divorce simultaneously. Practical approach and corrective measures will also be of immense help in maintaining conjugal bliss in spite of adverse planetary placement in the birth charts.

9

From the Astrologer's Desk: An Outlook on Case Studies

I shall analyse a few horoscopes with a view to highlight the marital status of their owners vis-à-vis the planetary potential in them. One is happily married to a noble, good-looking and highly educated girl. The other is still unmarried though he has crossed the 38th year. He even seems to have lost the urge for marriage. They both belong to good families, are handsome and living comfortably, but are poles apart in marital status. Why is it so? You can't say that it's simply a matter of chance. Marriage is an important event, and to believe that chance controls it, is unconvincing. The karmic factor is the answer, which is manifested though the planetary potential existing in the native's horoscope. Astrology is not a hoax. Rather it is a valuable science, having a twice-tested system. It helps us to discover ourselves.

The 7th Bhava, its lord and the Karaka, Venus rules marriage, the wife and marital bliss. *Phala Deepika* allots the Karakatwa of the husband to Jupiter, whereas Nadi Granthas take Mars to represent him. *Brihat Parashara Hora Sastra* surprises us by calling Venus (pati, husband).

These are likely to cause confusion and need to be weeded out. I am of the view that Venus and Mars deserve to be the Karaka of the husband, for he governs the sexual urge in a woman, besides being a close associate of the Moon in the matter of her menstruation. Jupiter is not stated to rule her sexual desires, and is, therefore, not qualified to represent her husband. Venus represents the native's wife and his seminal fluid. So he, too, cannot be the Karaka of husband. Mars does this job nicely.

BADHAKA RUINS MARRIAGE

Let us start with marriage. The 7th Lord is one of the planets bringing about marriage. The Kalatrakaraka Venus, whichever lordship he gets, is also to be counted as the second force bringing marriage. The benefic and friendly planets associated with the 7th lord or Venus and the lord of the 2nd House Kutumbasthana play a secondary role in solemnizing the native's marriage. This group becomes the third group of planets which can bring marriage. When the Badhaka afflicts one of the three sources of power, the remaining two groups may bring marriage resulting in failure of prediction of the Badhaka effect. If Badhaka is in a position so as to afflict all the three sources of power that assist in bringing marriage, the marriage will be inordinately delayed or denied altogether. This is a very rare situation.

This principle is applicable to all significations of life.

Mars in 6th House, Sun and Mercury in 4th House are malefic. Rahu in lagna on Sagittarius, Jupiter and Ketu in

7th House are also malefic, which does not promise family bliss and marriage is denied (see Chart 1).

Chart 1: D.O.B. 10.04.1955

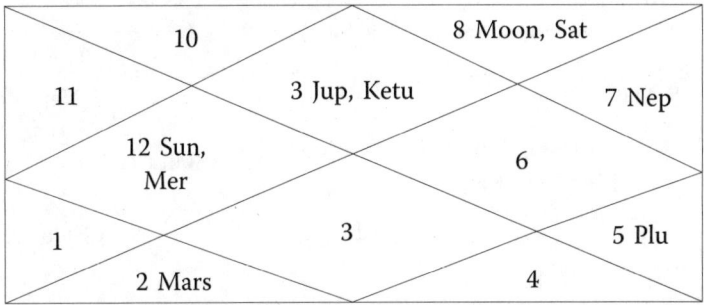

I have come across several horoscopes in which there are four or more planets in one House, yet most of them are married and have a comfortable life. When we go into the details, we find that they live as sanyasis at the mental level and live a materialistic life forced by circumstances.

The natural bent of mind of the native of Chart 2 is that of a sanyasi. The Lagna had entered Kumbha and so 9th lord Venus gets Badhakadhipatya. The 7th lord is the Sun and he is closely associated with Badhaka. Both together aspect the 7th Bhava by virtue of being close to the Lagna degree. The 2nd lord Jupiter is also close to them. Thus, 2nd lord, 7th lord and the 7th House have been afflicted by the Badhaka power. This man is a bachelor and marriage is denied altogether. If Venus had not been there with the Sun or if he were in retrograde motion or if the man were born about 10 minutes earlier making the Lagna Makara instead of Kumbha, early marriage would have been the result in spite of so many planets in one House.

Chart 2: D.O.B. 8.02.1926

	8 Moon, Sat		6
9 Mars		7 Asc		5 Nep
	10 Jup, Sun Mer, Ven, Ketu		4 Rahu
11		1		3 Plu
	12		2

Vain Longing

The Lagna is Taurus and Saturn becomes Badhaka in Chart 3. The Sun is the carrier of Badhaka powers of Saturn in this case. The 7th lord Mars through Vasi Yoga, Mercury occupant of the 7th House and Venus Kalathrakaraka through Vasi Yoga with Sun combine together. (Vasi-Ves is effective up to 60 degrees of separation). Kalatrakaraka Venus is also afflicted by Saturn independently by his 3rd House aspect. Thus, the Badhaka power controls 7th lord, 7th occupant and Kalatrakaraka.

Chart 3: D.O.B 9.11.1925

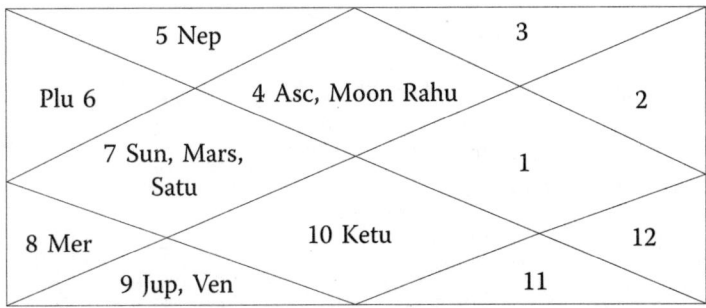

This man was forced into marriage during 1971. He did not live with his wife even for a single day. Subsequently, their marriage was declared null and void by a court of law. Till his last day in 1988, he craved for a life partner in vain.

In all the three cases, there is no strong force except Badhaka to deny or delay the marriage.

Separation from Spouse

A combination of natural malefic, Mars and Saturn in the 11th, 12th or 2nd House leads to some sort of rupture and finally dissolution of a marriage. I have observed this malefic result in many charts. Especially, when the Moon associates or opposes the combination of Mars and Saturn, the dissolution of marriage appears to be more certain. In Chart 4, the Badhaka effect is emphasized in causing separation or divorce.

Chart 4: D.O.B. 15.01.1954

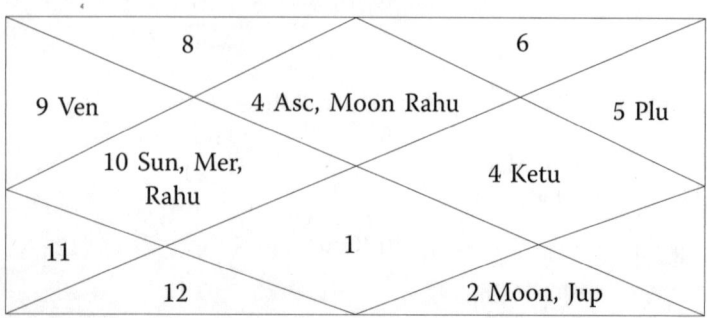

Except for the occupation of Badhaka in the 7th House, the lords of 2, 7 and 12 are well-placed and the houses 2 and 12 are free from any afflictions. The 7th Bhava is afflicted by Venus.

The Moon and Venus are just 1degree away from the optimum of 120degree ± 10degree for a perfect Trikona. The Moon aspects 2nd lord Jupiter. Thus, the 2nd House gets spoiled resulting in separation of husband and wife. They separated in 1982 or 1983, but divorce was not initiated by either side.

In the husband's chart with Kanya Lagna, Badhaka Jupiter aspects 12th Bhava (Leo) by being in Kumbha. Saturn is in the 12th in Log. This combination denies him conjugal pleasure signified by the 12th house. No other defect is seen in his chart.

Badhaka Moon is in (7th House) in Chart 5. The 7th lord and Kalatrakaraka Venus is in Lagna forming perfect opposition to Badhaka. The 7th Bhava is therefore completely spoiled. There are no benefic aspects on the combination.

Chart 5: D.O.B. 10.11.1946

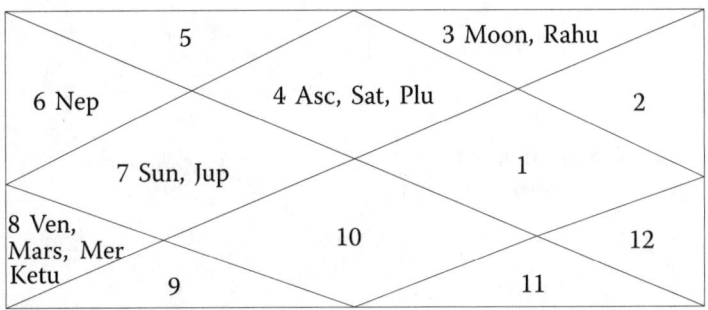

The native married and lived with his wife for only one day. Then they separated. No divorce was initiated by either side. They have only one boy as a result of their marriage and the boy is with the mother. This predicament cannot be attributed to any other malefic except for the Badhaka effect.

Elopement

The native of Chart 6 was employed. The husband was very pious and well employed. They have three girls, the eldest being 13 years old.

Chart 6: D.O.B. 10.11.1954

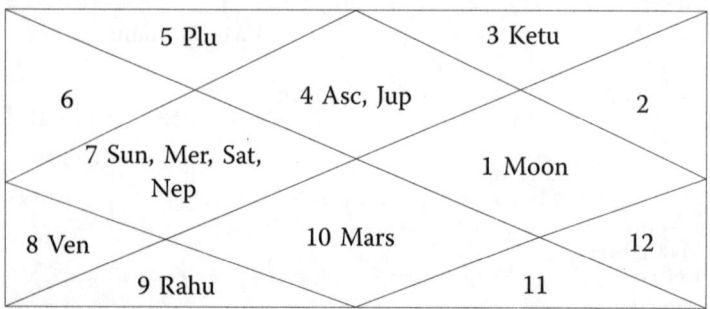

In July 1988, she eloped with a colleague along with the three children. Her whereabouts were not known except that she was later seen by some people at some place. The 12th House is absolutely spoiled by Badhaka. The 7th lord Venus is natal Venus, 7th lord in 7th from natal Moon. Ketu, the planet of spiritualism and salvation (Moksha) in transit catalyzes the religious momentum of the Dasa lord, thus making it adamant in its attitude of active participation in the construction of temple and other allied religious activities. The trinal positions of Jupiter and Ketu with radical Venus has accelerated its political position yielding it high status despite the collapse of state governments and polarization of all political parties against its ideology.

Saturn in Aquarius causes kantaka or ardhashtama due to its position in the 4th House from natal Moon. This transit of Saturn will not be helpful to the party.

As explained by Dr B.V. Raman, transit effects of Saturn from the 4th and 5th houses from the natal Moon are adverse. The party may get embroiled in internal conflicts and even split. Some leaders may come out of it or there may be bereavement of prominent leaders. According to *Phala Deepika,* the transit results of Saturn becomes fully effective in the last Drekkana of a Rasi. The party may suffer internal conflicts between March 1995 and June 1995 and also during December 1997 to April 1998, the 8th House transit of Saturn from radical Moon sign. Some serious setbacks are foreseen for the party. During the 6th House transit from May 1998, the party will prosper up to June 2000 by kneeling down its political opponents, particularly when in the last Drekkana (April 2000 to June 2000).

In the Bhukti of Rajayogakaraka Rahu after September 1997, excellent results may be experienced only during the favourable time of major planets. Taking into consideration the combined effects of favourable Dasa Bhukti and the major planets in transit, it can be predicted that the party may form the government at the Centre and several states in the country between March 2000 and June 2000. The above effect may promptly follow due to conjunction of Jupiter and Saturn in Aries under transit forming trine with natal Mars-Rahu-Jupiter-Saturn combination. The favourable Bhuktis of Sun and Moon may protect the party from disintegration expected to be caused due to adverse of Saturn, but the Mars Bhukti remains unsafe due to infighting and setbacks to party. At the start of Sun Antara in Sun Bhukti between November 1993 and January 1994, the party may face elections in four states, where its governments were sacked previously. The party may fail to retain all our states due to adverse transit of all major planets such as

Jupiter, Saturn and Rahu. The transit of planets has always had an important edge over the Dasa Bhukti results. Merely favourable Dasa Bhukti without favourable transit of planets can never fetch desired results.

Understanding Badhaka Planet

Spoiled by Adhiyoga with the Moon. The 2nd House is equally spoiled by Rahu, who is in a Trikona with the Moon. This happened during Mars Dasa.

Divorce

In Chart 6, the man married in 1964 has two boys and a girl. In 1981, they separated and in 1984, they were divorced. The Sun carries the Badhaka power of Mercury through Vasi Yoga. The Lagna and the Moon + Jupiter in 2 are also afflicted by Badhaka power. The 2nd Lord Saturn is coupled with Rahu by Trikona formation who, in turn, gets the Badhaka power through Ketu in a different route. Thus, the 2nd lord is independently influenced by Badhaka. The afflicted Jupiter in the 2nd spoils the Bhava and the 2nd lord gets afflicted through Rahu. Thus, the signification of the House is spoiled entirely and the home becomes extinct by divorce.

In Chart 7, lord of the 7th House, the Sun is exalted. Movable Stree Karaka is Jupiter (by virtue of having the least longitude in the sign) who is associated with a benefice Moon. Venus occupies the fourth a kendra. All the conditions are fulfilled. The native has one wife.

Chart 7: D.O.B. 26.04.1959 at 2.17

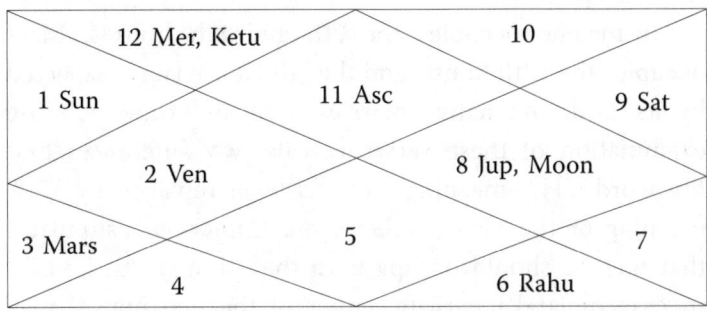

Second Spouse Yoga (see Chart 8): If Saturn is situated in the 8th House, the native marries a second time after the death of his first spouse or dissolution of marriage (divorce).

Chart 8: D.O.B. 22.10.1953 at 8.18.00

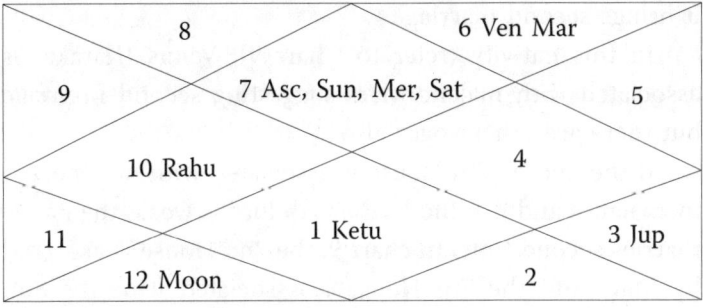

The above-said yoga is fully applicable when considered from the Moon who is powerful being full moon. Saturn is in the 8th House and Mars is the 7th House from the Moon. The girl had a second marriage after getting legal divorce from her husband and giving custody of two children to their father.

If malefic occupies the 7th and 8th houses. Mars occupies the 12th house, and the 7th House is not aspected by its lord, the native marries a second time. A close examination of these verses reveals two differences first the word CHA meaning and has been replaced by VAA meaning or the Verse in *Sarvartha Chintamani* stipulates that malefic should occupy both the 7th and 8th houses. In case of Jataka Parijata, either of the two houses may be occupied by malefic. Second, the word ADRISHAYA has been interpreted differently. Some say it means 'not aspected', others say it means situated in the 'invisible half' from the middle of first (house to the middle of 7th House)

If Karaka for wife is associated with malefic or occupies his debilitated sign or Navamsa, and aspected by malefics, it brings second marriage

In this nativity (refer to Chart 9), Venus (Karaka) is associated with malefic Mars suggesting second marriage but there are other yogas also.

If the 2nd or 7th House is associated with or aspected by malefics and the 2nd lord or 7th lord is weak, the native marries second time. In chart 9, the 2nd House is aspected by Mars and the 7th House is associated with the Sun Mercury lord of the 7th exalted in sign but debilitated in Navamsa

If the ascendant lord or the 7th lord occupies his debilitated sign or inimical sign or is combust or is in a cruel Shashtiamsha, the native married second time. In Chart 9, the ascendant lord Venus is debilitated and 7th lord Mars is situated in an inimical sign. In Chart 9, the 7th lord is in a cruel Shashtiamsha. We give another example.

Chart 9: D.O.B. 6.10.1944 at 18.30

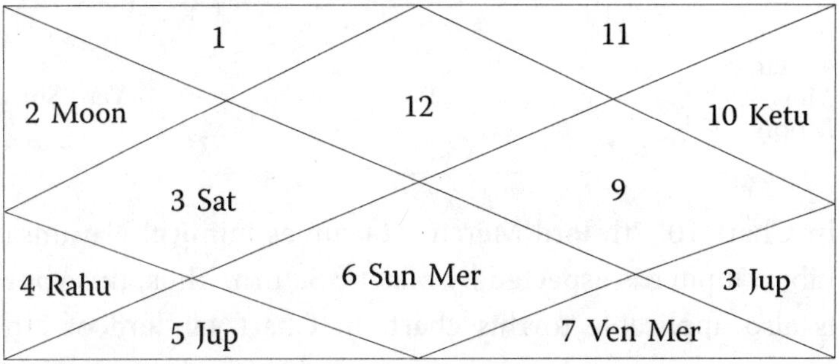

```
            1              11
  2 Moon        12              10 Ketu
         3 Sat         9
  4 Rahu       6 Sun Mer        3 Jup
         5 Jup        7 Ven Mer
```

In this nativity (Chart 10), the ascendant lord (Jupiter) occupies his debilitated sign Capricorn and is in a cruel Shashitiamsha. The native married a second time after the death of his first wife.

If Venus occupies a fixed sign in association with the Sun and Mercury and the 7th lord occupies a malefic sign, the native marries twice.

This yoga is fully applicable to the nativity discussed in Chart 10. Venus in Scorpio a fixed sign in association with the Sun and Mercury. The 7th lord is Mercury, who occupies a malefic sign (Scorpio).

If the lord of the Navamsa occupied by the 7th lord is in his debilitated or inimical sign/Navamsa or combust or hemmed in between malefics or aspected by malefics, the native marries second time.

Chart 10: D.O.B. 06.12.1914 at 13.30

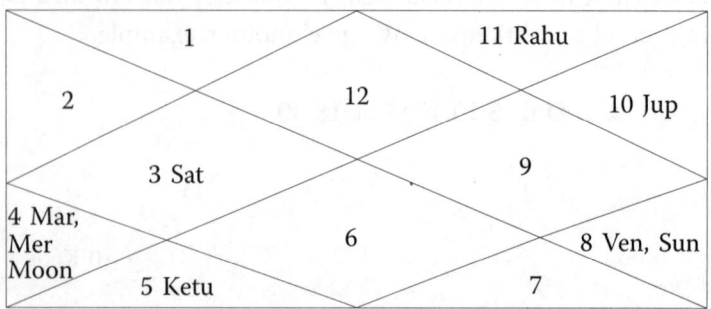

In Chart 10, 7th lord Mercury occupies inimical Navamsa Libra, Jupiter is aspected by malefic Saturn. Thus, this yoga is also applicable to this chart. In Chart 11, lord of 7th Mercury occupies Leo Navamsa ruled by the Sun. The Sun occupies an inimical Navamsa in Capricorn. Here also the yoga is applicable.

Venus occupies a moveable sign along with a malefic, second marriage is indicated. In Chart 10, Venus along with Mars occupies Libra, a moveable sign.

If the 7th lord is associated with Saturn or related with Rahu, the native marries twice.

In Chart 8, the 7th lord from the Moon is Mercury associated with Saturn. Saturn in turn is related to Rahu (being the dispoister of Rahu)

If the 7th lord associated with a benefic occupies an inimical or debilitated sign and malefics occupy the 7th House, the native marries twice.

In this nativity (Chart 11), Rule (1) described above is applicable. Mars occupies the 7th House. There is no malefic in the 2nd House, but it is aspected by Mars. Second Lord Venus is aspected by Saturn and associated with Rahu.

Chart 11: D.O.B. 15.06.1928 at 13.30

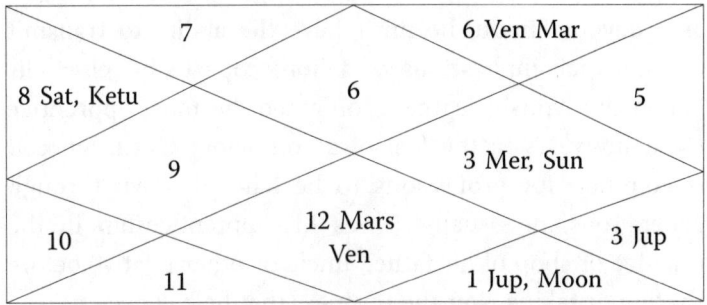

From the Moon, 2nd House is occupied by Rahu and the 7th House is aspected by Mars. The 2nd and 7th Lord Venus is associated with Rahu and aspected by Saturn. The yoga is fully applicable and the native married thrice. Their last marriage took place in February 1994 at the age of 66 years.

The Role of Astrologer in Fixing a Marriage

A book about Hindu astrology would be incomplete without a more definitive description of the Hindu astrologer and the invaluable services he provides. His influential and multi-functional role of therapist, medical practitioner and, at times, priest has earned him utmost praise and respect within the Hindu community.

In order to maintain a commercial practice, an astrologer must possess an in-depth knowledge of astrology–or a degree–on the complicated study of the precise mathematical and astronomical principles of the heavenly bodies, which sometimes take up to eight years to complete. Although he may never use every facet of this study, the astrologer must nonetheless have the knowledge of them all, while, as a devout Hindu, he must have the ability to transmit the spiritual implications of a horoscope to his clientele. When the jyotish degree is obtained, he must apprentice for many years in the feet of a competent Guru. Since it is common for professions to be handed down through generations, he usually serves his apprenticeship in the practice or shop of his father, uncle or other relative before sharing or taking over the business that he has been geared for since childhood.

In addition to the astrologer's position in the community as general seer, confidante and therapist, he is also the source of sacred knowledge.

In ancient times, the astrologer believed he had a direct line to the gods, that his words had a divine source, that he was an intermediary who transmitted sacred teachings. Although there are some religious gurus in India who teach meditative techniques and others who profess to have the ability to heal and the power to bless, it is the astrologer who, like the priest or rabbi, provides non-judgemental and wise counsel. His astrological sessions are, at times, 'confessionals' furnishing comfort, hope and encouragement in bleak moments. Unlike his Western counterpart, the Hindu astrologer serves the community and is available for advice whenever needed. Modern young Hindus do not always visit an astrologer for accurate lifelong prediction as their parents did. Instead, they seek him for unbiased advice, or simply to discuss their problems. If they leave less burdened, their visit was worthwhile.

Perhaps the astrologer's most significant duty towards his community is sanctioning marriages, still mostly prearranged by the parents and one of the most important decisions a woman and man must make. As is the case with many contemporary religions and cultures whose ancient traditions are still practised, Hindu matrimony is not merely the marriage of two individuals, but the union of two families.

Families who do not have prospective partners in mind must search for another family with whom to unite. Sometimes they may consult an astrologer who will advise them as to the profession, age, caste, and even in which direction to search. If the daughter's or son's chart reveals that the marriage partner lives to the east, the astrologer advises them to search in places located east of the child's birthplace. If the west is indicated, they are advised to look west of the birthplace. The search for a suitable marriage partner may take place by word of mouth, business or family connections or by means of a newspaper advertisement, a very common practice in India.

Acknowledgements

At the very outset, I would like to offer my thanks to my guru, Swami S. Chandra ji, who made it possible for you, the reader, to hold this book in your hands.

Smriti and Arun (a couple in America) got married after the consultation of an eminent astrologer. Marriage was solemnized after proper matching of horoscopes with proper mahurats and auspicious time. Despite all these, they had been leading a very unhappy married life. They were childless. For that, they would visit priests, astrologers and deities but with no result. They were on the verge of separation when they visited me. Totally disturbed and depressed, they became my followers. They were compatible with 23 scores, but the position of Venus and Mars was not benefic. There was existence of Mahapatak Dosha and Guru Chandal Dosha, which was responsible for disturbed marriage. I performed some upayas and they were able to save the marriage and were even blessed with a child in 2003. This instance brought me acclaim and a huge clientele from different parts of the world.

I acknowledge my thanks to Smriti and Arun, whose horoscope study encouraged me to write a book on matching of horoscopes. There is already a large number of books on astrology, but I felt none of them really did elaborate work on individual planets—the basic root of the increasing rate of divorces and infidelity in conjugal life.

Marital bliss is an experiment in fusing the life of one into the life of the other which could teach the partners how to merge in the universal consciousness.

My wife, Poonam, and my sons, Ayushmann and Aparshakti, and their respective wives Tahira and Akriti, who made it possible for me to lead a fairly normal life and be a successful astrologer.

My heartfelt thanks to all my friends, whose unconditional love and emotional support eased my adjustments to a strange way of life and who made the writing of this book a joyous task.

I thank Ishaa Wadhwa, Kushpreet Kaur and Subhash Kumar for their hard work, devotion and efficient management of my work schedule and office.

Last but not least, I express my thanks to Shri R.K. Mehra, director, Rupa Publications, New Delhi, for his most valuable contribution to make this work a complete and wholesome success.

P. Khurrana
www.astroindia.com

DELHI	CHANDIGARH	MUMBAI
+919810349900	+919914699900	+919769449900